Pay Dirt

"Buy on the fringe and wait. Buy land near a growing city!"
— John Jacob Astor, America's first multimillionaire

Pay Dirt

**How the Individual Investor Can Bank Land for Great Profit
and Avoid Shams, Scams and Worthless Real Estate**

By Darren K. Proulx

Land Resource Investments, Inc., P.O. Box 50163, Sparks, Nevada 89435

Library of Congress Control No.: 2005939096
ISBN (hardback): 0-9777801-3-9
ISBN (paperback): 0-9777801-2-0

Publisher: SuccessDNA, www.successdna.com
Editor: Michael Sion, www.mikesion.com
Page designer: Milan Sperka, www.meshcreative.com
Cover illustrator/designer: Ron Oden, www.ronoden.com
Cartoon illustrator: Jeff Hickman, www.chops.com/hickman
Cover concept: Jillian R. Proulx
Printer: Sheridan Books, Ann Arbor, Michigan

First edition

Published in the United States of America

Disclaimer

Neither the author nor the publisher is providing legal, investment, tax or accounting advice. The author and publisher specifically disclaim any liability resulting from the use or application of the information in this book. The reader should seek the services of a qualified professional for all legal, investment, tax or accounting advice.

"Pay dirt"

Something very valuable or very useful that is found after searching or effort.

"Landbanking"

The process of buying and holding land for future sale or development.

To my good parents, wife and children.

And to all who recognize that land can secure their family's future.

Contents

Acknowledgments

Many people are involved in the production of a book. I can't thank everyone, but here is a list of some key contributors:

My daughter Jillian, who created the cover design concept; Mike Sion, for his tireless hours of editing; Garrett Sutton, Esq., for his legal and publishing expertise; Jeff Hickman and Ron Oden, for their artistic prowess; Milan Sperka, for his fine page design; Patrick McDonnell, for his proofreading; Richard "Dick" Ramsey, for his innovative concept that allowed this small investor to create wealth in land; George R. Kucera, Esq., for providing his expert legal counsel over the past decade; and Ron Kemper, Jim Tatum, Pat Sheehan and Ken Bogart, for sharing their landbanking experiences.

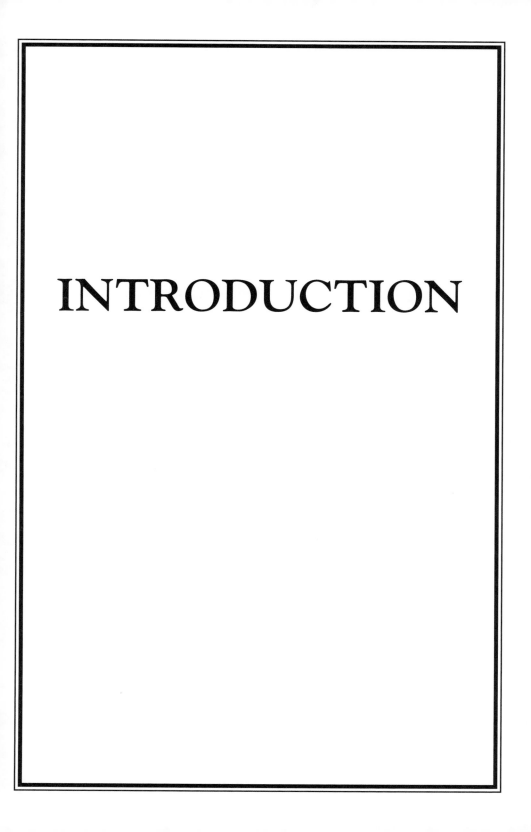

INTRODUCTION

If you're looking to get into buying land, you may get shown something really far out.

INTRODUCTION

My ill-fated first investment in land

I 'll never forget the first piece of land I bought. I was 21 years old, and eager to start building my fortune. Not surprisingly, I didn't have much clue how to go about doing that. But I didn't let this stop me from trying!

I'd graduated from high school in Riverside County, California, three years before and was dishing up ice cream for a company that had food-service contracts at stadiums and convention centers. I figured I had a spark of entrepreneurialism in me; so while keeping my day job, I branched out with my own freezer and sold ice cream from booths at community fairs.

Anxious to get my meager savings working for me, I religiously scanned my local newspaper's classified-advertisement section for investment opportunities. What I was most interested in was real estate. I was after a hot piece of dirt. And this was largely due to my father's influence.

My father, you see, was a licensed general contractor who'd been building homes in Southern California since the end of World War II. Throughout my childhood and adolescence he'd regaled me with stories of the population boom that had transformed Southern California; he also frequently bemoaned his own missed investment opportunities. For example, when our family would visit the Knott's Berry Farm theme park in the city of Buena Park, we'd drive down Beach Boulevard, the old Highway 39, and my father would remark, "You know, I used to drive down Beach Boulevard and there was nothing on it." Back in the 1950s and early '60s, my father said, he'd drive for miles and miles on the boulevard, passing farmland and open space until he reached the beach. Now, a transformation had taken place. I'd marvel at how many businesses, homes and public facilities lined each side of the four- to six-lane metropolitan thoroughfare.

Similarly, my father would mention residential lots that had sold in yesteryear in Newport Beach or Huntington Beach for $2,500 or so. I'd ask him why he hadn't bought some of that land in what were now pricy markets in upscale Orange County. His answer: "It takes two things at the same time, and I never had 'em at the same time: forethought and money." Sometimes he'd had extra money to invest — but not the vision for how an area was going to explode in growth and drive up real estate prices. Sometimes he'd had the insight — but not the cash.

I vowed to myself I'd learn from the missed opportunities my father had shared with me. With the earnestness of starry-eyed youth, I resolved that I wouldn't miss out on land-investment opportunities. No sirree. Instead, I'd employ brilliant foresight and get lucky — despite my tender years, almost nonexistent savings and utter lack of experience from which true foresight stems. None of that deterred me. I knew there was no better time to start accumulating my first million than the present. So I kept scouring the classified ads for my first score.

One day I came across a tiny ad that said:

Calif. real estate
Low payments. $100/month.

Heart pumping, I called the phone number at the bottom of the ad. A man we'll call Burns answered. In a seasoned voice that was friendly and casual, Burns told me the property was in Adelanto. I knew that was a small town out in the desert. Burns arranged to meet me out on the state highway past Adelanto's city limits. A Joshua tree would be the landmark.

"We'll jump in my car and I'll show you what's going on," he said.

I suddenly felt very adult.

I pulled up at the appointed spot at the appointed time. Sure enough, Burns was waiting there, sitting in a shiny, silver, late-model Lincoln Continental. Very professional. He climbed out and shook my hand. He looked like a nice, well-off guy in his 70s. A grandfatherly type with slicked-back white hair, leisure suit, bolo tie and cowboy boots.

As we drove out into the open expanse of the Mojave Desert, Burns chatted about the property and handed me photocopies of newspaper articles. The photocopies were faint (copies of copies) and the articles were from a good number of years before, but this didn't faze me. The clippings touted the great potential of the area outside Adelanto — how it would see intensive residential development — and mentioned the costs of subdividing the lots into 2½-acre parcels. Burns noted that the price he was asking for each of his lots was lower even than what it would cost to subdivide them. In other words: He was offering a terrific deal.

We drove for what seemed to be a long time before Burns pulled off the highway. I checked my watch. The property was a good half-hour drive outside Adelanto. It felt like the middle of nowhere: a lonely sweep of hill and sand, Joshua trees and bramble bush. This was jackrabbit country, dirt-biker paradise. Still, for vacant desert, it was kind of nice, up on a little bluff. Burns' lots had been graded by tractors at one time, and the outline of where a street would go was faintly clear.

"It's a long-term investment," he said with a nod.

As I surveyed the barren terrain, I allowed my newfound powers of foresight to kick in. I imagined neat whitewashed adobe homes with pink-tiled roofs rising against a clear blue sky; manicured yards of cacti, fountains and gravel bordering a circle of smooth blacktop glistening under the bright desert sun. Children playing. Dogs barking. It felt so good to dream!

I took a special fancy to a lot where a cul-de-sac was planned. The price seemed right to me: $8,995. The down-payment was $700. The rest would be paid via a coupon book at the rate of $102 a month. I did some calculations in my head. Even on my meager earnings, I could swing it. The bug had bitten deep. It was all I could do to maintain a poker face.

I told Burns I'd think about it. The next week, I drove out with him again. I ended up buying the lot on the future cul-de-sac. I signed a land contract. In this contract, the buyer pays for the property but doesn't actually own it until having paid out a certain sum, at which time the seller transfers the deed of ownership.

In the years that followed, I kept paying on the property. There were months I was hard-pressed to come up with the $102 for my precious piece of dirt in the sticks. Sometimes I'd miss a month and make it up with a double payment the following month. I also paid $60 or so twice a year in property tax. That tax bill would give my wife the opportunity to question me about my foolish investment.

But I stubbornly held onto the property . . .

Would you be surprised to learn that my lot on the future suburban cul-de-sac in desert paradise never appreciated in value? That's because never did a developer come along who was interested in acquiring the property to actually build something on it.

The value of my parcel never went up. San Bernardino County eventually bought up the lots to use as a public park for dirt-bike trails. I was paid $5,000. That was less than I'd paid for the property, not even including the interest. In the final analysis, it had been a crummy investment.

My obligation to write this book

DOES THIS STORY SOUND familiar? I'm not surprised if it does. Perhaps you've suffered a similar experience, or know someone — a relative, friend, neighbor or coworker — who has. That's because today nothing has changed much in the land-selling business.

Properties in the boonies such as the one I bought when I was 21 are regularly identified and acquired by unscrupulous opportunists, hyped up in promotions and then unloaded on unsuspecting, inexperienced small investors. These worthless plots of dirt are churned on the market, often sold back to the opportunists by the buyers after they've given up and settled for a loss . . . or even have lost the properties due to unpaid property taxes — after which the tax assessor forecloses on the lots and sells them at auction, where the opportunists can snatch them up for cents on the dollar. Then the properties are resold by these same opportunists to a whole new crop of innocent small investors whom these slick salespeople count on to exploit.

You may not be surprised to learn — as I eventually did — that Burns had been a land promoter for some big companies, and part of his compensation from his employers was the lots out in the Mojave Desert he'd been selling. In fact, years before I'd met him, Burns had sold these lots to other green investors, then taken them back in foreclosure after the investors had realized what they'd gotten into and decided to quit making their monthly payments and cut their losses. In his waning years, Burns had decided to sell those lots all over again. That was the point at which I — eager to employ my "foresight" — had responded to his little ad.

"Land developer" conjures up a fast-talking swindler peddling worthless swampland. The negative stereotype is a pity because good investments are out there to be had by people who know what to look for — and what to avoid.

Scams such as the one I fell for have given land development a bad reputation in financial circles. The phrase "land developer" conjures up the image of a fast-talking, jewelry-draped, cologne-reeking swindler peddling worthless swampland in Florida. This is very bothersome to me, because I have made land development, in the form of landbanking, my career. The negative stereotype is also a pity because good investments that yield tidy profits are out there to be had by people who know what to look for — and what to avoid.

That's why I'm writing this book. It's from a sense of obligation. For in the 17 years since I first got my shoes dirty acquiring that initial plot of worthless desert soil, I've learned the game from the ground up. After trying various occupations

— ice cream scooper and vendor, carpet cleaner and car repo man, process server and newspaper deliverer, owner of a business applying anti-graffiti coating to signs and walls — I worked with my dad on a few of his home-building projects and earned my contractor's license. I became a "paper contractor," subcontracting out work to build homes. Later, I worked for a private lending company making construction loans, and learned that side of the business.

Today, I'm president and CEO of Land Resource Investments, Inc., a landbank-development company incorporated in California and headquartered in Sparks, Nevada (next to Reno). My business is finding quality "pre-development" (empty or agricultural) land in Southern California and elsewhere in the western United States to buy up and "bank" — that is, hold onto until it's the right time in the market to sell the land, for profit, to a builder, developer or investor.

After I find an attractively priced parcel that is strategically located in the path of imminent urban growth, and is accessible to nearby utilities and infrastructure, I'll buy the parcel. I receive title to ownership in the parcel and earn a profit after the landbanked parcel reaches its maximum appreciated value, and the parcel is sold — typically to a land developer. The developer, in turn, builds commercial, industrial or residential projects.

You may be unfamiliar with the term "landbank." It's a phrase I first learned from my own mentor, Richard "Dick" Ramsey — an experienced real estate investor. It was my great good fortunate to have Dick take me under his wing when I was in my late 20s, and give me the education that elevated me from an eager but naïve real estate investor to one capable of recognizing a good deal from a poor one, and able to buy and sell at the right time.

To hit "pay dirt," you might say.

My education to write this book

WHEN I MET DICK, I still owned that dusty, lonely parcel of Mojave Desert a half-hour drive from the nearest town. By this time I was 29. Through connections from my construction-lending job and my side career as a home contractor, I was introduced to Dick, who was in his 70s and a consultant for a land-development company. Dick was very accomplished at what he did. His strategy was to have clients buy acreage in the path of urban growth and hold it for future use or sale. Dick hired me to build houses on a piece of land that one of his land-development clients had.

One day, Dick and I were driving in the vicinity of my little investment. I decided to impress him. I pointed out the window and said I owned 2½ acres on that little bluff ahead.

Dick started quizzing me about the property. Does it have infrastructure? Does it have water? Does it have sewer? Does it have power? Are there paved roads nearby?

Very quickly, I grew embarrassed.

It was at this point that my education in land investment really began.

Through Dick's tutelage, the scope of my folly became crystal clear. I saw that the property I purchased from Burns was too far from any power grid to justify the expense of bringing in electricity. Similarly, it was too remote from sewer and water lines. So much for the property being "in Adelanto." (Indeed, a common ploy of land hucksters is to reference the nearest city when describing worthless real estate. "Only 25 miles from [name your city]!")

Dick started instructing me on what it takes to have a viable piece of property for development. He showed me some of the properties he was involved in. These parcels were right where residential or commercial growth was ripe, on the outskirts of expanding urban areas. This made me very envious, and also desirous to participate in such golden ventures. Right away I saw the difference between just buying land, hoping it would appreciate in value and become attractively salable at some unspecified date in the future, and intelligently banking land, accumulating acreage in the path of growth with a clear strategy of selling it as soon as the numbers were right. What Dick's clients were doing was "banking" land.

Dick also taught me that it wasn't the buying of good land at a low price that made for a smart investment — it was selling the land at the right time for a good profit. (This is why landbanking may not be the best option for investors looking for a quick flip, and whose timetables don't allow them to wait five, seven or 10 years before selling and realizing a profit. But it is an excellent option for most

---

Landbanking may not be the best option for investors looking for a quick flip, and whose timetables don't allow them to wait five, seven or 10 years before selling and realizing a profit. But it is an excellent option for most investors who are at least 10 years from retirement and can afford to wait the necessary period.

---

investors who are at least 10 years from retirement and can afford to wait the necessary period.)

Characteristically, wealthy investors don't fall prey to scam dealers — the Mr. Burnses of the world — because wealthy investors are usually more sophisticated, and also can afford to buy properties closer to urban areas, where land is far more likely to appreciate in value than remote areas where the real estate is significantly cheaper. It's the small investors who have a rough time finding good land to buy!

A few years after I met him, Dick and I decided to implement an ownership concept that would allow individual investors to come together and buy the sort of valuable undeveloped real estate usually only available to the purchasing power of big investors, such as large corporations. In 1999, Land Resource Investments, Inc., was born.

The lessons Dick taught me and the expertise I've gained over the past 17 years is what I'm sharing in this book. It's knowledge that can greatly benefit you if you aim to capitalize on wise land investments.

After I discovered the dire need for a new book on investing in land, I toyed with the idea of writing a book myself. It took me quite a bit of time before committing to the project, but I finally did. The result is in your hands. It contains the information I wish I'd had back when I was 21 and starting out on my own search for pay dirt.

Most major newspapers carry ads every day selling land that is not fit for landbanking. Like the ad I responded to when I was 21.

Had I had this book back then, I'd have saved paying $102 a month for a long, long time!

Now you're ready for *your* education

NOW WE'RE JUST ABOUT ready to begin your education in finding and investing in pay dirt. Allow me to explain how this book is structured. There are 12 chapters, divided evenly among three parts:

- Part I, "The Benefits of Landbanking," explains why land is valuable, what landbanking is, and telltale signs of scams to avoid.
- Part II, "The Power of Landbanking," goes into depth about the unique concept of landbanking — how it works and why it works, and how to ensure it will work right for you.
- Part III, "The Profit of Landbanking," walks you through the advanced stages of owning a landbanked parcel — watching its value mature, preparing to sell it — and selling it for gain (which is the whole point of the endeavor — and the best part of it!).

Read the book once, absorbing what you can, then reread it.
And keep it handy as a reference guide.

I've deliberately kept this book short, written to the point. I want the information to be as easily digestible as possible. I applaud your willingness to spend time and effort learning the essentials of landbanking. To make matters even easier for you, I've encapsulated key points of each chapter at the end of that chapter.

My recommendation is that you read through the book once, absorbing what you can, then reread it a second time. And as you move ahead in actually investing in land, it's not a bad idea to keep this book handy as a reference guide.

I fully believe that if you apply the lessons learned from the book's 12 short chapters, they will prove practical — and profitable. And after you hit "pay dirt," please feel free to contact me at the email address listed in the back of this book and share your success story. Not only will it give me great satisfaction to hear from you, but I just may seek your permission to reprint your story in a subsequent edition of this book. Your story could help inspire more small investors to gain the knowledge necessary to find prime land to invest in and hit pay dirt themselves.

Let me close by borrowing an analogy my dad used:

"Smart investing is like baking a cake."

Think about it. You have to have the right ingredients, and combine them at the right time and in the right order, to get your cake to rise, and be edible and delicious.

If you don't have all the ingredients, or if you don't mix them correctly, you'll go hungry.

A thorough reading of this book might not make you a master baker right away, but it will give you the recipe you need to become one.

The rest comes down to time spent in the kitchen.

....

PART ONE

THE BENEFITS OF LANDBANKING

Savvy wealth-seekers have pursued good land throughout history.

CHAPTER ONE

Land: Secure and Stable

T he late American humorist Will Rogers, whose homespun wisdom gained him national celebrity in the 1920s and '30s, has a famous quote attributed to him: "Buy land. They ain't making any more of the stuff." In truth, these words are a paraphrase of the following quip the Oklahoman made in 1930 about investing in California beach property: "Out here I had been putting what little money I had in ocean frontage, for the sole reason that there was only so much of it and no more, and that they wasn't making any more."

But the principle, however it's worded, remains true: *Good land is limited.* Therefore, it's a natural resource for investors.

Many wealthy people hold a fair proportion of their wealth in real estate. It's how they balance their portfolios among the many other kinds of investments, such as stocks, bonds and business interests. Holding and accumulating wealth by owning land is as old as civilization itself. It's proved itself for millennia to not only be "good as gold," but even *better* than gold. This is because land is

---

Holding and accumulating wealth by owning land is as old as civilization itself.

---

finite, while it's always uncertain how much gold can be mined (and geologists are always searching for new lodes and trends in the far corners of the globe). What's more, good land isn't subject to the volatile market fluctuations for commodities such as precious metals, or securities such as stocks and bonds. Land is reliable. Historically, it's the path to wealth.

It was true in biblical times. It was true in the middle ages. It is true today. Consider the following quotations from famous people of recent centuries past:

"It is a comfortable feeling to know that you stand on your own ground. Land is about the only thing that can't fly away."
— Anthony Trollope, English novelist (1815-1882)

"Real estate is an imperishable asset, ever increasing in value. It is the most solid security that human ingenuity has devised. It is the basis of all security and about the only indestructible security."
— Russell Sage, American financier, railroad and telegraph mogul (1815-1906)

"Buying real estate is not only the best way, the quickest way, the safest way, but the only way to become wealthy."
— Marshall Field, American department-store pioneer (1834-1906)

"Real estate cannot be lost or stolen, nor can it be carried away. Purchased with common sense, paid for in full, and managed with reasonable care, it is about the safest investment in the world."
— Franklin D. Roosevelt, 32nd U.S. president (1882-1945)

When it comes to land value — as Will Rogers knew when he invested in beachfront California soil — *location* is important. Consider these quotes:

"Buy on the fringe and wait. Buy land near a growing city! Buy real estate when other people want to sell. Hold what you buy!"
— John Jacob Astor, fur trader, capitalist, America's first multimillionaire (1763-1848)

"Every person who invests in well-selected real estate in a growing section of a prosperous community adopts the surest and safest method of becoming independent, for real estate is the basis of wealth."

— Theodore Roosevelt, 26th U.S. president (1858-1919)

"Land increases more rapidly in value at the centers and about the circumference of cities."

— William E. Harmon, real estate developer and philanthropist (1862-1928)

In sum, then, investing in well-situated real estate is a secure, stable and historically proven method for building wealth. The value of good land ever increases — providing long-term capital appreciation. In fact, land can outperform the returns on stocks by a significant extent; good land also outpaces inflation.[1] Land also lends itself to sources of investment income not available for other investments, such as stocks, since banks and other lending institutions are interested in making loans on investments that are tangible.

And what is more tangible than solid dirt? You can touch it, feel it, stand on it.

It's visible for all to see. If you own stock, you probably don't even have a certificate saying you own it. What you likely have is a number recorded at a brokerage, and a transaction printout you can keep on file. But if you own a good piece of land in the path of growth, not only can you visit it, but it's very likely that you eventually will receive unsolicited letters in the mail from agents or investors interested in buying the land from you.

I look at it very simply: If you own land and keep up with your property taxes, it can't be taken away from you.[2] A stock or other paper asset can decline in value due to the vast array of market forces, or due to directors' mismanagement. But

---

[1] One of the main reasons a sum invested in real estate can outperform the same sum put into stocks or bonds is due to the power of leverage, which will be discussed more in Chapter Seven.

[2] The Fifth Amendment to the U.S. Constitution says, in part, "nor shall private property be taken for public use, without just compensation." Thus, even a governmental bid to acquire private property, under the concept of eminent domain, requires the payment of fair market value.

real estate is a hard asset, like the chair I'm sitting on.

Every investment entails a degree of risk. With land, there are realistic and unrealistic risks. An example of an unrealistic risk is the emergence of a sinkhole. Another example is a devastating earthquake. (A cursory pre-purchase investigation of the potential for such calamities destroying a piece of land should suffice to eliminate concern for such unrealistic risks.)

Realistic risks with real estate relate to market forces — such as a significant decline in an area's employment, or a drop in population — depreciating the value of a piece of land. But a wise investment in a growing area may be as close to a sure bet as exists in the financial world.

To repeat Franklin Roosevelt's quote from earlier in this chapter:

"Real estate cannot be lost or stolen, nor can it be carried away. Purchased with common sense, paid for in full, and managed with reasonable care, it is about the safest investment in the world."

The population explosion creates pressure for good land

When I was born, the human population of our planet was just under 4 billion. As I was writing these words 38 years later, the population had reached approximately 6.5 billion, and was continuing to increase, including in our own nation. Six decades ago, America had about 100 million people. The post-World War II baby boom and continuous heavy immigration are two key factors behind the near tripling of the U.S. population from 1945 to today.

California, especially, exemplifies the exploding population. In 1950, the Golden State numbered about 10 million people. A half-century later, the total was triple that. California's population is about 36 million as I am writing this, and projected to reach between 42 million and 48 million by 2020.[3] Interesting,

---

[3] Figures come from the California Department of Finance, the U.S. Census Bureau and the Public Policy Institute of California.

however, is that only 18 percent of California's 101 million acres is developable, according to that state's Department of Fish and Game. (The remaining 82 percent

---

In any area with a surging population, the pressure builds up for land development — for housing and businesses, parks and schools, infrastructure and services. It's supply and demand.

---

is designated as wild land, such as mountains, deserts, tributaries, wetlands, and so on.) What's more, 14 percent of the land that's available for development already has been developed — leaving only 4 percent of raw California land as developable.[4]

Let me offer one more quote by a famous person — in this case, British statesman Winston Churchill (1874-1965): "Land monopoly is not the only monopoly, but it is by far the greatest of monopolies — it is perpetual monopoly, and it is the mother of all other forms of monopoly."

In any area with a surging population, the pressure builds up for land development — for housing and businesses, parks and schools, infrastructure and

---

Tremendous opportunities exist for small investors to enjoy significant returns on land. Yet most Americans never consider investing in real estate beyond their own homes.

---

services, and so on. That translates into a steady appreciation in the values of land, including undeveloped land in the path of growth outside urban areas. It's simply a matter of supply and demand.[5]

Tremendous opportunities exist for investors, including small investors, to enjoy significant returns on land. Yet most Americans never seriously consider

---

[4] According to the Center for Continuing Study of the California Economy.

[5] A classic book on landbanking is *The Simple Truth about Western Land Investment*, by Leland Frederick Cooley and Lee Morrison Cooley. Published in 1964, with a revised edition in 1968, its wisdom about the principles behind landbanking are as sound today as they were four decades ago. Here is what the Cooleys said about what they called "people pressure": ".. . since we continue to make more people but cannot make more land, people pressure must drive land prices upward as demand increases for living and recreational room." The Cooleys will be quoted several more times in this book.

investing in real estate beyond their own homes.

Securities — stocks, bonds and mutual funds — are extremely easy to purchase nowadays, especially through on-line brokerages, and are easy to research on-line or through more traditional sources, such as at libraries or through mass-circulated newspapers and magazines. Finding good land takes a bit more digging. It takes research and patience. And it takes know-how.

But the rewards can be phenomenal. And they are within the grasp of any ordinary person who commits the effort.

Reading this book can be your first step toward moving yourself out of the masses of unwilling or uninformed investors who shy away from buying land. This book is aimed at investors who care to take the time to learn the principles of finding good land. And who are committed to putting their capital into that land.

Just as Will Rogers did. Just as investors from time immemorial have done. Just as I have done. And just as you can, too.

KEY POINTS TO REMEMBER:

- ☛ There is always plenty of land to buy. But good land is limited. Therefore, good land is a natural resource for investors.
- ☛ Historically, land ownership is the path to wealth.
- ☛ Land increases more rapidly in value at the centers and about the circumference of cities.
- ☛ Good land can significantly outperform stocks, and outpaces inflation.
- ☛ Pressure builds up for land development in any area with a surging population. Property values appreciate, including for undeveloped land in the path of growth. It's simply supply and demand.
- ☛ Tremendous landbanking opportunities exist for investors large and small, but most Americans never invest in real estate beyond their own homes.

Inflation's negative force hasn't been able to stem the appreciation in valuable land.

CHAPTER TWO

Inflation: The Silent Thief That Can't Lift Land

A U.S. dollar in 1970 bought a lot more than it did in 2000. In fact, it was worth $4.44 in 2000 dollars, to go by the most often-used measure of comparison, the Consumer Price Index.[6] A dollar in 1950 was worth $7.15 in 2000 dollars.

All this is due, of course, to inflation — the rise in the cost of goods; or, to look at it another way, the fall in the spending power of currency.

Again using the CPI, inflation was rising at 1.05 percent a year in 1950, by 5.94 percent in 1970 and by 3.38 percent in 2000. (The peak annual rate during that half-century was 13.48 percent in 1980; the valley was -0.31 in 1955, meaning there was actually deflation. But that was the only year out of 50 in which deflation occurred.)

The rise in the cost of living is obvious in society itself. The norm for the American nuclear family used to be one income provider per household. Since the 1970s, the norm for these families has been a two-income household. Another bit of obvious evidence: The smallest unit of exchange, the penny, has just about lost its significance in our monetary system. You can pick up a few of them for free

---

[6] The CPI, compiled by the U.S. Bureau of Labor Statistics, is based upon a bundle of goods and services, such as food, housing and transportation, used by the average household.

to make exact payment at the counter of your local convenience store — or drop the coins into the counter's penny container after receiving a few of them in your change, to avoid the nuisance of carrying them around. Nickels or even dimes can sometimes be found on counter containers, too.

Investors try to keep ahead of inflation. They want their rate of return to exceed the rate by which the currency falls in value. If inflation is at 3 percent a year, the investor wants an annual return above that, or the investor will be — in effect — losing money.

The good news for investors in land is that good land traditionally appreciates in value faster than inflation. The reason may be that consumers cannot get by without land. They can get by without luxury items. They can economize when it comes to transportation (taking public transportation or

---

Good land appreciates faster than inflation. Consumers can economize in many areas of their budget, but will always need a home to live in. Businesses and governments always need space. Where population is growing, demand for well-situated land is constant.

---

car pooling instead of driving a car). They can manage their budgets in a number of areas. But they will always need a roof over their heads, and space for their home to sit on. Similarly, businesses will always need a physical place from which to do business. Governments will always need space for police and fire departments, administration buildings, schools, post offices. If an area's population is growing, then more homes will have to be built, and more space created for the retailers and service providers to meet the needs of the new residents.

In an area where population is growing, the demand for well-situated land is constant. The steadily increasing value of land may very well be a factor, itself, in the rising cost of living.

Residential land prices increased by a factor of 10.4 — meaning they became more than 10 times higher — from 1970 to 2003.[7] The increase is surely one of the factors behind the 73 percent rise in U.S. housing prices from 1997 to 2005.[8]

The population increases; good land outpaces inflation

AS I WAS WRITING these words in mid-2005, the monthly rate of inflation was 2.53 percent, well within the range of the past five years. The yield of the Standard and Poor's 500 stock index — comprised of 500 of the largest U.S. companies, and commonly used by financial experts as a benchmark for the overall U.S. stock market — was 2.06 percent for the previous 12 months. That means that in general, the stock market was lagging slightly behind inflation, losing money for investors during this period.

Markets, of course, fluctuate, as does the inflation rate. The economy is never static; it ebbs and flows, advances and retracts, with various sectors moving in different directions.

But if there's one piece of sound investment advice, it is this:

Since the nation's population continues to expand, the nation's economy will continue to grow. And more land will be needed for development to accommodate the increase in population and economy. Therefore, good land will continue to rise in value, higher than the increase in the cost of living, greater than the decrease in purchasing power of currency. And good land is a surer investment than the stock market as a whole.

Inflation, the silent thief, won't be able to siphon the wealth from the good earth.

KEY POINTS TO REMEMBER:

☞ The U.S. dollar has been declining in value for the past half-century, due to

---

[7] From the study, "The Price and Quantity of Residential Land in the United States," by Morris A. Davis, of the Federal Reserve Board of Governors, and Jonathan Heathcote, of Georgetown University.

[8] Article, "In Come the Waves," in *The Economist*, citing multiple sources, June 16, 2005.

inflation. But good land traditionally appreciates in value faster than inflation — and may even contribute to inflation.

🕳 People cannot get by without good land — for homes, businesses and public services. In areas with growing populations, good land becomes ever more valuable.

🕳 In the mid-2000s, inflation was outpacing the stock market. But residential land prices were increasing much faster than the inflation rate.

Before buying land miles from nowhere, make sure the factors are in place that "somewhere" is on its way.

CHAPTER THREE

What Is Landbanking?

"**L**andbanking" is the process of buying and holding land for future sale or development. Landbanking is just one of the many methods of investing in real estate.

One of the trends among small investors as I am writing this was buying rental properties — apartment houses, duplexes, single-family residences, trailer parks, storage units, commercial office space, and so on. Many books have been published in the past five years about this strategy.

Landbanking — as the hybrid word itself implies — means banking land. It doesn't involve tenants and cash flow. It isn't about taking over a going concern. Unlike with rental properties, there are no clogged toilets or garbage disposals to attend to for tenants. There is no financial statement — projecting anticipated income, expenses, vacancy factor and cash flow over a future period — to review on a property being considered for purchase. Landbanking is a speculation. But it is a speculation based on solid evidence.

The whole goal of the landbanker is to buy undeveloped land that will appreciate in value to the point at which a buyer will come along and offer a price that represents a reasonable profit. The land typically is empty ("raw," "undeveloped" or "unimproved" — all synonyms) or agricultural land. The buyer may be a builder of a residential subdivision, or a developer of a retail complex.

The buyer may be a governmental entity that needs the land for schools or parks. The buyer even may be another investor.

But landbanking is different from just buying undeveloped land. Remember the desert-baked bluff a half-hour out of the nearest town that I bought a 2½-acre parcel on when I was 21? That was an example of just "buying land." I put no research into the market. I wasn't even aware how to go about researching the market — or even that this was a necessary step! While I told myself I was getting into the real estate game, and would make a handsome killing on my parcel after a homebuilder came along one day in the hazy future and created a neat cul-de-sac, maybe I mostly wanted to feel like a landowner.

In contrast, "landbanking" entails finding undeveloped land that meets the criteria of a sound landbanking investment, so that it will yield a profit upon

---

Plenty of people buy a plot out in the middle of nowhere and think they're landbanking. But they've failed to check whether key ingredients are in place to attract developers.

---

resale. Why do you put money into an interest-bearing bank account? So that it will be protected, and so that it will grow. Putting your money, instead, into your mattress, or having, say, your brother-in-law hold onto it for you, is a different deal. It's not really banking.

Now, there's nothing wrong with just "buying land" for your own personal interest. Maybe you have a dream of building a home on the land someday. Maybe you want the land for fishing, hunting, hiking or camping on. Maybe it would be a nice place to garden.[9]

But "landbanking" is all about investing — buying and holding a piece of land in the path of growth with an eye on selling it at the right time. And this

---

[9] One clever entrepreneurial company, The Lunar Embassy, sells one-acre parcels on the moon. For $31 (as of this writing), the buyer receives a parcel on the side of the moon facing Earth, plus a lunar deed, lunar site map and "Lunar Constitution Bill of Rights." This certainly isn't landbanking, but it's kind of a romantic little purchase, isn't it?

— to repeat from the book's introduction — is why landbanking may not be for investors looking for a quick flip, whose timetables don't allow them to wait five, seven or 10 years before selling and realizing a profit.

Landbanking involves doing legwork. The true landbanker may scan the same promotional ads for undeveloped real estate that lure average everyday folk (as we will discuss in Chapter Four), but the true landbanker sees those promotions only as a small part of the market survey. Landbanking is not gambling on land. Landbanking is taking a diligent, thorough, educated approach to finding and buying empty land, with the clear intent of holding onto it until the market is at the right point at which selling the land makes financial sense.[10]

There are plenty of people who end up buying a plot out in the middle of nowhere and think that by doing so they're landbanking. But they've failed to check out whether the key ingredients are in place to eventually attract developers and make the plot valuable. (The key ingredients will be discussed in chapters Five and Six.) These naïve investors really aren't "landbanking." They're merely buying land. There's a difference. Yet there seems to be an endless supply of these hope-filled investors, stumbling blindly in the dark. Even buying land site unseen.

That's the reason I'm writing this book!

KEY POINTS TO REMEMBER:

☛ The goal of landbanking is buying undeveloped land that will appreciate in value and inevitably attract a buyer to yield a profit.

☛ True landbanking involves research — buying land that meets the criteria of a

---

[10] The Cooleys, authors of the 1960s classic *The Simple Truth about Western Land Investment*, suggested that investors drive around their own growing hometown to see new areas. Surprises are certain to await, they said. "Subdivisions, tracts, shopping centers, out-door theaters, golf courses, parks, playgrounds and what-not spring up so fast these days that you simply lose track of them." The Cooleys hastened to add that each of these developments stand on land that once was inexpensive, and perhaps even considered not worth much. But whoever had the good sense or fortune to hold onto that land long enough probably reaped a rich sum.

sound investment. This is different from just buying and holding undeveloped land, or acquiring land for recreational use.

🔑 Since a number of years may have to pass before undeveloped land appreciates significantly in value as urban growth approaches, landbanking may not be for investors with shorter investment timetables, looking for a quick flip.

Paradise peddlers, including fading stars, can capitalize on investors' fears about Social Security and the stock market to lead them to far-off, risky real estate.

CHAPTER FOUR

Scammers, Sharks and Suckers

I n Chapter Two I mentioned that residential land prices have soared in the United States in the past 35 years. They're more than 10 times higher than in 1970. I also gave the statistic that U.S. housing prices shot up 73 percent from 1997 to 2005. It shouldn't be surprising, then, that a multitude of small investors has flooded the real estate market.

It's ever the same throughout history. If word spreads that gold has been discovered in a far-off land — a gold rush is triggered. (And pity the latecomers and the greenhorns who risk all for nothing.) When the U.S. stock market, buttressed by the dot-com mania, boomed in the late 1990s, investors poured in. Then they got to experience what a bubble felt like after it burst.

Legendary circus impresario P.T. Barnum is credited with the famous saying, "There's a sucker born every minute."[11] When it comes to land speculation, suckers are in endless supply. There is nothing new under the sun. The Cooleys, authors of the 1960s classic *The Simple Truth about Western Land Investment*, dubbed unscrupulous land promoters as "Paradise Peddlers." Swindlers selling swampland in Florida is a cliché; but Florida swampland

---

[11] Actually, a Syracuse, New York, banker named David Hannum uttered those words, angry that thousands of spectators were paying to see Barnum's Cardiff Giant (reputedly a fossilized giant man, but actually a figure carved from gypsum), when Barnum had only had Hannum's giant copied.

is still being sold. Land-fraud schemes abound in the United States — and, indeed, around the world.[12]

This is not to make light of small investors lured by the returns to be gotten from land. The attraction is clear in any era; and as I am writing this, the reasons why ordinary Americans were looking more hungrily at the land market included their uncertainty about the stock market, and concerns over the health of the Social Security system. A *Los Angeles Times* article printed in March 2005 noted the trend of middle-class Californians liquidating stock portfolios and retirement funds and even taking out second mortgages on their homes (which had shot up in value), "pouring the money into real estate, often in distant states, often without seeing the property."[13] The article led off with the story of a 58-year-old insurance agent from a San Francisco Bay area suburb who'd sold off most of his mutual-fund shares and plunked down $83,500 for a 10-acre lot in the hills south of Reno, Nevada, that a real estate agent had recommended and shown him a photograph of. The investor was eager to buy the land because he was favorably impressed by the Reno area's strong, steady growth. When he finally visited the site that he was sinking money into, he found it to be on more precipitous terrain than expected. There also were "a lot of rocks. Big rocks," he told the *L.A. Times* reporter.

Hopefully, the buyer was able to either terminate the sale before it was irrevocable, or — if he did finish purchasing the property — there would be a happy ending and the steep, stony acreage would turn out to be a good investment for him. ("I've got a good feeling," he told the *L.A. Times* reporter.) But thousands upon thousands of other inexperienced land investors are burned every year. My own initiation, as I described in this book's introduction, was at the hands of a kindly older gentleman hawking worthless desert soil. (Fitting, isn't it, that I've changed his name to "Burns"?)

---

[12] As one example that land fraud respects no international borders, the Melton Borough Council, in the East Midlands region of England, issued a consumer warning in 2004 about an unscrupulous company advertising and selling agricultural land that the company made to seem was approved as residential land. The scam did not violate existing laws. A council staff member said the company bought the land for £3,000 per acre and was marketing half-acre and acre plots for up to £35,000 per acre.

[13] "Putting Stock in Property," *Los Angeles Times*, March 27, 2005.

There is a lot of work — "due diligence" — to be performed before a careful investor puts money down on a piece of land. (It still surprises me that some people will still put more research into buying a used car than they will investigating a piece of land, as if real estate investments are influenced by sheer faith.) These necessary steps of due diligence will be described in Part II. But just as important is the screening phase: knowing what kind of property is worth researching, worth investing one's precious time on — and what deals should be immediately avoided.

Eight classic red flags

HERE ARE EIGHT OF the classic red flags to watch out for:

1) **Short length of ownership.** If the owner has held the property for a relatively short period of time, such as only a year, why is the owner interested in flipping the property so quickly? Is there a major problem with the property (say, inadequate zoning, or poor soil) that had gone undetected before the previous purchase? There may, however, be legitimate reasons — such as inheritance — that the seller has owned the property only a short time.

2) **Seller himself should be interested in developing the property.** If the owner is, say, a homebuilding company, shouldn't it be building on the property instead of selling it? Are there shortcomings with the property that you need to find out?

3) **Property seems too cheap.** If the price per acre is much lower than the market warrants, then it's very possible the land is just not worth much and the seller is trying to get whatever possible for it.

4) **Property is part of a large development in a foreign country.** First, the economic, legal and political stability of a foreign country can be questionable. Landowners and investors are vulnerable to such realities. In contrast, the U.S. legal system provides a number of protections to the buyer, including property rights and the ability to buy title insurance. Second, the ability to travel to,

and perform due diligence on, a property in a foreign country is expensive and problematic. Third, if you buy, say, one of 7,000 lots in a Mexican resort area, how can you expect the resale value to go up? For starters, you'll be competing with all the other buyers, and there's always someone more desperate than you to sell, and at a lower price. It's a supply-and-demand issue. What's more, developers can be building many more units in the area, so that increases the buyer's market. Remember: There is plenty of land-investment opportunities right here in the United States.

5) **"Three hours from Denver."** A common tactic in property advertising is trumpeting how close lots for sale are to growing, dynamic or prominent areas. Even remote plots of dirt at enormous distances from paths of development — and whose only likely future residents are jackrabbits, mosquitoes and other native fauna — can be made to seem as choice parcels right in the thick of things. I sometimes collect these ads out of in-flight magazines. I marvel at the descriptions: "Only 45 minutes from Taos"; "SW of Albuquerque, NM";

Typical pressure tactics of scammers include making it seem that a line of buyers is waiting for the very opportunity the clients being shown the site have.

"Ski resorts within 1½ hours from property." I smile, too, at the swaths of pristine, undeveloped (and undevelopable) land depicted in accompanying photographs.

6) **"Mountain views."** A variation on the "Three hours from Denver" is touting an area's rustic beauty: "In the heart of nature"; "Untouched beauty"; "Mature tree cover"; "Gorgeous grasslands"; "Mule deer and bear roam the forest." And as with the "Three hours from Denver" ads, photos of gorgeous, unspoiled (and unbuildable) land typically are included. (Remember, if you're buying property as an investment to landbank and sell to a developer, it's different from buying property to enjoy for your personal recreation use.)

7) **A high-pressure, fast-paced real estate agent or land seller.** Typical pressure tactics of scammers include making it seem that a line of buyers is waiting for the very opportunity the clients being shown the site have. A scammer might arrange for a confederate to make a phone call during the visit, and the scammer — within earshot of the clients, of course — can say into the phone something along the lines of: "No! I'm about to show that lot. You tell them that it's not available. But if my good guests who are right here decide not to take it, it's available to them starting tomorrow."

8) **Highly promoted, non-governmental land auctions.** Often held at hotels or convention centers, tuxedo-clad auctioneers sell parcels to the highest bidders. The properties on the auction block usually have been bought at tax sales for pennies on the dollar. Consider that the previous owners likely let the properties go to foreclosure because they weren't worth paying the taxes on.

Also consider that the auctioneer does not guarantee that the land is buildable or even has adequate zoning. There may even be homeowners' association fees or special bonds assessments for the buyer to pay. All sales are final.

A quirk of human nature is that we believe facts, but trust our emotions. But buying on sheer optimism is bad to do in any kind of investment.

Four emotional pitfalls

HERE ARE FOUR OF the emotional pitfalls for investors to avoid:

- **Buying on sheer optimism.** This is a bad thing to do in any kind of investment. But it happens time and again. A quirk of human nature is that we believe facts, but we trust our emotions. And guess which we are more prone to act on?

    Consider the middle-aged San Francisco Bay area insurance agent, mentioned earlier, who'd gotten interested in the Reno area because of what friends, articles and Internet sites were saying about Reno's growth (which, indeed, is remarkable). Unfortunately, that's where his research stopped — finding a good area. He didn't then research a good piece of land in that area. While driving around the area he stopped to ask questions of a couple walking a dog, and the woman happened to be a real estate agent. She signed him on as a client, he shelled out $83,500 (that had been in his retirement accounts) for 10 acres, and only after the sale's paperwork was finished and the deal was in its final stage did he actually visit the site — and discovered it to be on a grade steeper than imagined, and strewn with boulders. To his credit, he decided to have a local builder check out the property before the deal was final. Still, the investor said, "I'm willing to bet it's going to work out. *I've got a good feeling.*"

So do thousands upon thousands of other investors who put their hard-earned savings into land far, far away — land they never even visit, but which gives them a "good feeling" because it looks good to them in the photograph.

- **Buying without visiting a property.** This goes without saying! Some investors may resist visiting a property because they subconsciously don't want the vision in their minds to be tarnished by the reality of what a property actually looks like. They'd rather maintain their happy dream. Don't you be one of them!

- **Buying without completing a thorough investigation.** An investor needs to allow himself/herself enough *time* to perform due diligence. That includes visiting a site, but also its surrounding area to see whether the site truly lies in the path of growth and development. Consider allowing yourself a few days to poke around and explore.

A smart investor should hire appropriate engineers and other experts to thoroughly examine a property, and should check with local governments about master plans and zoning (again, we'll discuss due diligence in more depth in Part II). But if an investor gets lazy about research, or succumbs to a rush to buy under pressure from a salesperson, then the proper due diligence cannot be performed, and the investor will be almost flying blind.

Remember: If a property is bought for landbanking as an investment (as opposed to for personal recreational purposes), it has to be attractive to a builder or developer in the future.

- **Buying to get rich quick.** Again, this is a bad thing to do in any kind of investment. Buying to get rich quick is related to buying on sheer optimism. Salespeople can trumpet all kinds of statistics showing how real estate yields phenomenal returns, and how a certain piece of dirt is certain to skyrocket in value within a short period. Vacant land is especially attractive to many investors because, unlike rental properties, empty land requires no continuous hands-on management. And small investors on the lookout for undeveloped land see plenty of examples in their everyday life of an empty lot on which a convenience store or

---

"Antiquated subdivisions" predating modern zoning, and left for dead by their original developers, are still out there, and being sold by hucksters.

---

other business is suddenly being built. The investors think: "Why didn't I move on that lot before it went up in value?" *Shoulda, coulda, wish I woulda.*

This all-to-common non-buyer's remorse can manifest itself in an unfortunate way. The investor starts projecting potential onto other empty lots for sale, imagining to the point of blind faith that they will soon be snatched up by developers eager to build convenience stores or strip malls. These empty lots represent a quick fortune-in-the-making to the investor.

But successful landbanking, as we will discuss in Part II, is rarely a matter of buying property then quickly turning around and selling it. Successful landbanking almost always is a matter of employing a slow, intelligent, calculated strategy. Timing is critical. And timing, well, takes *time.*

Beware of over-the-hill actors pitching old, overpriced lots

THE 1960S WERE THE heyday of land scams, when thousands of buyers were duped by beautiful advertisements showing pristine forested lakes, sparkling new communities and golf courses. What many of these victims actually bought were lots in undeveloped, remote areas ranging from rolling, scrubby foothills to seas of sagebrush to bone-dry swaths of desert sand. Eventually the age of modern zoning laws dawned as local governments required developers to provide sewer and water, power and other infrastructure before gaining approval to subdivide land.

But the so-called "antiquated subdivisions" predating modern zoning are still out there, grandfathered in under the laws. And guess what? Parcels within these left-for-dead subdivisions are still being sold. Even if the original developers couldn't unload them, and gave up, there are opportunistic companies willing to buy them up cheap to foist upon unsuspecting investors (of which, per the quote attributed to P.T. Barnum, there is a never-ending supply). One of these companies even hired as its sales spokesman an actor whose face and voice are familiar to both English-speaking and Spanish-speaking television fans in the United States: Erik Estrada, who gained fame playing the character of a California Highway Patrol motorcycle cop named "Frank 'Ponch' Poncherello" in the late 1970s and early '80s NBC-TV show *CHiPS*. Estrada later played a role on a Spanish-language soap opera shown in the United States and Mexico on the *Univision* network.

"Ponch," no longer a hunk but sporting a paunch, still carried enough star power to interest the opportunistic real estate company to have him as its pitchman. The company has sold lots in subdivisions abandoned by their original developers in California, Florida and Washington state. One subdivision, California Pines, sits amid the high-desert hills and flats of northeast California. "This place is gorgeous!" Estrada exclaimed in television infomercials for California Pines. Yet a mountain lake shown in an ad for the development is actually 30 miles away, while the lake within the development itself was described by an Associated Press newspaper reporter as "a muddy cattle reservoir that shrivels in the heat." Fewer than 400 houses stand on the 15,000 platted lots in remote and economically depressed Modoc County.

The Modoc County treasurer told an interviewer with the *National Enquirer* supermarket tabloid (whose interest was obviously kindled by faded actor Estrada's participation in the land promotion) that she received telephone calls each month from unhappy land buyers. A San Francisco Bay area church leader told the AP reporter she had paid more than $64,000 for four lots that would probably sell on the open market for only $3,000 to $6,000 apiece.

Incidentally, Estrada's employers, the two partners in the real estate company, have been in some legal hot water related to land advertising. In 2000, Santa Cruz County, California, prosecutors sued a different company of the partners, alleging false advertising for a subdivision called Happyland, whose mountainside lots had been platted in the early 20th century. Buyers complained they couldn't even find the sites because the roads on maps didn't really exist. The company denied that nothing could be built on the land, but settled the lawsuit out of court and offered refunds to buyers who requested them.

In 1992, another of the partners' companies ran newspaper ads for condominiums in Santa Monica, California, promising ocean views and showing pictures of the beach. The Santa Monica city attorney's office accused the company of false and deceptive advertising. The company admitted no wrongdoing, but quickly settled and agreed to a permanent injunction and the paying of costs and penalties.

As part of Estrada's compensation for doing the infomercials for the real estate company, he was given a lot in each of the subdivisions he advertised. Therefore, he was telling the truth when, after piping, "This place is gorgeous!" in the California Pines promotions, he continued: "Take my word for it because I own property there myself." When questioned by the AP reporter, Estrada said he had no plans for building on any of the lots the company had given him.

Protection — and tips — from Uncle Sam

THE PREVALENCE OF LAND-FRAUD schemes led to federal legislation to protect consumers. The Interstate Land Sales Full Disclosure Act, passed in 1968, requires full disclosure of all material facts in the sale or lease of 100 or more lots (with certain exemptions) through the U.S. Mail or interstate commerce. (Offerings of 25 to 99 lots, with certain exemptions, are also subject to anti-fraud provisions.)[14]

Under the required full disclosure, developers of non-exempt lots who sell or lease undeveloped land through the U.S. Mail or interstate commerce must provide every purchaser or renter with a property report before any contract or agreement is signed. The property report itself is required to provide key information about the property, such as who owns the property, the property's exact size in square footage or acreage, the tax valuation of the property, the zoning on the property, distances from the property to nearby communities over paved or unpaved roads, current and proposed utility services and charges, and soil and foundation conditions that could cause construction or septic-tank problems. (Know, however, that the federal government does not inspect lots or prepare or verify the contents of a property report. So the buyer should carefully review the information and question anything that doesn't look right. A recourse for a buyer duped by false information in a property report is filing a complaint with the U.S. Department of Housing and Urban Development's National Office of Interstate Land Registration. A wise course before buying a property, however, is to check whether any complaints against the developer are on file with HUD.)

Here are some commonsensical tips, which should *not* be ignored, from HUD and from the U.S. Postal Inspection Service:

- Visit the property. Never buy any land site unseen.
- Get the property report. Never sign a receipt for a property report until you have received and read it.
- Research the land. Review and check the elements in the property report. Ask if the developer has registered the subdivision with HUD; if it isn't registered, determine whether the subdivision qualifies for an exemption.[15]

---

[14] The U.S. Department of Housing and Urban Development's website address is http://www.hud.gov/. You can follow the links to "Land sales" for more information on the Interstate Land Sales Full Disclosure Act or on buying land.

[15] This applies, of course, only to developers. You may just be buying a vacant lot from its owner, an individual like yourself.

- Check for truth in advertising. Ensure that amenities and utilities touted in advertising materials are also listed in the property report.
- Get comps. Contact real estate agents in the property's area and obtain comparative prices ("comps") for similar plots of land nearby.
- Research the developer. Call the office of the state attorney general, the area's Better Business Bureau, and HUD, and ask if any complaints have been filed against the developer.
- Never rely on verbal promises. Have promises included in the contract terms.[16]
- Never sign any papers until you have read and understood them.
- Never succumb to high-pressure tactics. These include pitches in person, over the phone or from advertising materials.
- Never be tempted by pitches that seem too good to be true.

The postal inspector delivers a caveat

THE U.S. POSTAL INSPECTION Service begins one of its consumer-warning information sheets with the following two paragraphs, which make for an appropriate buyer-beware caution:

Whether you're looking for an investment, a vacation home or a place to retire, you need to exercise caution before buying a piece of land. Attractive real estate brochures in the mail may indicate the land is in a warm and hospitable climate with recreation and conveniences nearby.

However, if you don't personally see the land, you may later discover too late that it is in the middle of nowhere, far away from utilities and other amenities, and cannot be resold for even a fraction of the price you paid.

If only more people heeded this warning, then certain ex-TV actors, as well as hucksters, would have to find a more noble way to earn a living!

---

[16] In my experience, a broker typically hands you, the potential buyer, a written statement that says that any promises not in writing haven't been made. Therefore, if a broker claims that the municipal sewer line is a mile from the property, you need to get that put into writing. That gives you legal recourse should the claim about the sewer prove incorrect after you've bought the property.

A Sample of Letters to the Editor of a Newspaper, from Investors

I am publisher of *Land Investment News*, a quarterly newspaper founded in 1968 and covering the Southern California areas of Antelope Valley, Victor Valley and their vicinity.

The newspaper regularly receives letters and emails from readers. Below are two typical ones. The writers' names have been omitted, and identifying details deleted.

The first email is about land in a subdivision in a promising community:

I am from Guam and I also have 2½ acres of land located on 199E and N2 which I have not seen. Can you tell me anything about that area? I would really appreciate it and thanks for your good work.

This investor committed a typically unfortunate error. He bought the property site unseen. Had he visited the site, he would have found it was about 20 miles from the closest development.

This next email describes, unfortunately, the type of result characteristic for investors who rely on verbal promises:

All the expansion in Palmdale and Lancaster is great but what about the people who were sold land on _____ _____ Road in _____ for $7,000 an acre with no hope of ever benefiting from it in this lifetime? This was sold to me by ___ _____, a friend (?), back in 1981. He told us a 6 ft. water duct was going to be built out to ____. Well, duh! Never happened. We were rooked and now have no recourse. I guess where there are suckers there will always be hucksters.

A Latin phrase is appropriate to state here: *Res ipsa loquitur.* Meaning: The thing speaks for itself.

KEY POINTS TO REMEMBER:

☛ Unscrupulous land promoters take advantage of the endless supply of naïve investors, just as opportunists swindle marks in other rackets. As the old saying goes, "There's a sucker born every minute."

☛ Among land schemes are the sales of lots in antiquated subdivisions — those abandoned by developers (often in the 1960s) because they were too far from a path of urban growth, but which have since been bought by promoters, repackaged and put on the market again, sometimes promoted in infomercials.

☛ Uncertainty about the stock market and about the health of the Social Security system has drawn a fresh supply of investors into real estate.

☛ Good land takes work to find, but many investors put more effort into researching the purchase of a used car.

☛ Land-fraud schemes abounded in the 1960s, but still persist. Federal laws require disclosure of all material facts in the sale or lease of 100 or more lots (with some exemptions) through the U.S. Mail or interstate commerce, while offerings of 25 to 99 lots are also subject to anti-fraud provisions. Developers of these subdivisions must provide a property report before any contract or agreement is signed.

☛ Eight red flags for buyers considering property for sale:

1) The owner has held the property a short time.

2) The owner is a builder or developer yet not interested in building on the land.

3) The price is low for the market.

4) The property is part of a large development in a foreign country (resale is problematic and different laws apply).

5) The property is advertised as "three hours from Denver" or by a similar time reference to a well-known locale (indicating it could be extremely far from a path of urban growth).

6) The property is advertised with "mountain views" or a similar reference to natural beauty (indicating it could be wild, undeveloped country extremely far from a path of urban growth).

7) The seller or agent is high-pressure and fast-paced.

8) Highly promoted, non-governmental land auctions with fast-paced sales.

☛ Four emotional pitfalls to avoid:

1) Buying on sheer optimism.

2) Buying without visiting a property.

3) Buying without completing a thorough investigation.

4) Buying to get rich quick.

☛ Ten tips from the U.S. Postal Inspection Service, and U.S. Department of Housing and Urban Development:

1) Visit the property.

2) Get the property report and don't sign a receipt for it until you have read it.

3) Review the elements in the property report and ask if the developer has registered the subdivision with HUD or another government agency. (If not, determine whether the subdivision qualifies for an exemption.)

4) Check that amenities and utilities advertised are in the property report.

5) Get comparative prices ("comps") in the area.

6) Check whether complaints about the developer are on file with the state attorney general, Better Business Bureau or HUD.

7) Have any promises included in the contract terms.

8) Don't sign papers until you have read and understood them.

9) Don't succumb to high-pressure tactics.

10) Don't be tempted by pitches that seem too good to be true.

PART TWO

....

THE BENEFITS OF LANDBANKING

*Empty land in the path of urban growth, within eyeshot of development,
won't be empty for long.*

CHAPTER FIVE

Location, Location, Location And Timing, Timing, Timing

Knowing *where* to buy and *when* to buy are critical to successful landbanking. These two factors — *location* and *timing* — largely determine which properties you'll be interested in exploring as investments.

Here's a key to finding a property in a prime location at a prime time: Determine that urban sprawl is destined to reach the location within three to 10 years. Developers (likely busy building on land along a path of growth heading toward the property in question) have yet to snatch up the property; but you can bet wisely that developers will want to buy the property in good time, and at a price that will yield the owner a profit.

The term "urban sprawl" carries a negative connotation. It conjures visions of cookie-cutter residential subdivisions, retail centers with big box stores, and fast-food restaurants blending into each other, eating up rural pasture and cropland, forests and wetlands, and crawling up the sides of foothills. The image is of a sea of houses and streets, strip malls and office parks — soulless suburban neighborhoods distinguishable from each other only by their numbered freeway exits.

Environmentalists and "smart growth" advocates deride urban sprawl as a phenomenon rooted in developers' greedy quests for extra profit, and in homebuyers' selfish desire for extra living space, each with a disregard for the husbanding of limited natural resources. Critics say urban sprawl results from inefficient urban planning. Sprawl increases motor-vehicle traffic and air pollution, destroys green space, crowds schools — and even boosts taxes, since the scope of public services must be expanded (including building roads to reach suburban areas, which decreases the amount of taxable land).

But others see urban sprawl as a natural demographic phenomenon — the result of citizens' yearning for an improved quality of life and the American Dream, coupled with sheer population growth in an urban area. They cite the steady influx of residents into U.S. urban areas (driven by births among baby-boom era mothers, as well as heavy immigration to the United States plus high birthrates among immigrants). They argue that people will always crave and seek lower-density living areas with better schools, less crime, minimized noise and ambient light, and more overall privacy and room to breathe.

How one defines "urban sprawl" can depend upon one's view of it. One definition I've seen calls urban sprawl "a pattern and pace of land development in which the rate of land consumed for urban purposes exceeds the rate of population growth and which results in an inefficient and consumptive use of land and its associated resources."[17] Contrast that with the simple definition in *Webster's Ninth New Collegiate Dictionary*. *Webster's* cites the phrase as dating to 1961. The definition: "The spreading of urban developments (as houses and shopping centers) on undeveloped land near a city."

Whatever side you take, it is clear that the vast majority of urban growth in the United States as well as in Canada, the United Kingdom, Australia and Japan has been in suburbs in the past few decades.[18] Someday the trend may be reversed, and perhaps cities will tend to expand upward, with high rises,

---

[17] The definition comes from the website http://chesapeake.towson.edu, maintained by an organization called Chesapeake Bay & Mid-Atlantic from Space. The organization is concerned that "imperviousness" (the inability of water to infiltrate into soil, due to the pavement, rooftops and compacted soil related to development) "directly affects the environmental quality of streams and their watersheds."

[18] Statistics supporting this come from Demographia, an organization describing itself as "'pro-choice' with respect to urban development." Its website is www.demographia.com. Using figures from the U.S. Census Bureau, Demographia reports that the population in the major U.S. urban areas (core cities plus suburbs) from 1950 to 2000 increased by 347.3 percent. Demographia also reports, using national census data, that from 1965 to 2000, suburbs captured nearly 115 percent of urban growth in major Western European urban areas.

rather than outward. In that case, landbank investors will need to adapt to the changing landscape.

But at present, as in the past half-century, urban sprawl is reality. And developers will continue to create a demand for empty property in the path of a city's growth.

Builders compete madly to find good land

LAND DEVELOPERS COMPETE WITH each other, and the big cost variable in their field is affordable land in good, growing markets on which to build. Consider that builders pay essentially the same prices for construction materials: concrete, drywall, roofing, painting, plumbing, and so on. Builders pay essentially the same rates for subcontractors to put up houses and buildings, parking lots and landscaping, and so on. But builders *do not* pay the same prices for land. Finding good land is where the game is really played. The hunt is always on for good, cheap land a few minutes outside of town.

If you're driving out of an urban area and see houses going up on land where, only a few years or even months before, livestock was grazing, you can bet that a developer did the math about the area's population growth, housing demand and overall real estate market, and saw an opportunity to pick up ground cheaper than within the city. The developer calculated that homebuyers would be willing to drive an extra 10 or 20 minutes into town from a house outside of town, in order to save money on a home purchase. You can also bet that another developer is looking for even cheaper land even farther from the city limits on which to build even less-expensive houses.

This is how, in a few short years, a longtime resident of a city can be amazed at new subdivisions dotting the landscape that had been empty of human habitation and had always seemed just a long way out of town.

But the demand was there. Developers don't enter a market unless there is demand for the product. Developers anticipate the demand, staying just ahead of it, and helping sustain it.

The task of the landbank investor is to stay just ahead of the developers.

Narrow the field to mid-size, growing cities

SO HOW DO YOU locate a good city (or outskirts of a city) in which to landbank? It sounds like an enormous chore, doesn't it?

The good news is you can dramatically narrow your search by eliminating major cities from the search. The reason is that property there is usually too expensive. Property in and around these cities has been on the market for a long, long time, and therefore the prices have risen too high. What's more, property taxes usually are relatively steep in major cities, because the taxes are based either on a property assessment, or the price the buyer paid for the property. So any developer who buys property there must quickly build on it and sell the product before the property taxes eat him alive.

What you are looking for are growing, medium-size cities or towns within practical commuting distance to major cities. These medium-size communities are often thought of as "bedroom communities." Residents work, shop and go to restaurants and cultural and sporting events in the nearby big city, but enjoy the quieter (and more affordable) lifestyle in their suburbs. The growth in these suburbs may be driven by the exploding population in the overall metropolitan area, with residents pushing out to the suburbs. Or the growth could be fueled by an influx of retirees from elsewhere, seeking a better climate, or from residents from nearby states or regions seeking a better way of life due to economic or lifestyle pressures back home.

As long as the essential elements — including buildable land, sufficient water, a strong and diversified regional economy, and local government that is not anti-growth (and preferably pro-growth, approving building permits, and working to secure its supply of water and other essentials for the future) — are in place, an aggressive demand for homes and businesses in the medium-size, outlying community should exist, and continue.

In short — you are looking for a suburban area where more and more people want to live, and where builders can build the homes for the people who want to live there.

It takes some research to find such an area. To repeat from two paragraphs above: You can eliminate areas known to: lack outlying buildable land; be facing water shortages; have an unstable economy or struggling chief industry/employer; be administered by an anti-growth government, especially one that has instituted, or threatens to institute, building moratoriums.[19]

You are looking for areas that have positives in each of the above four categories. When I've identified one or more of these areas in which to hunt for landbanking property, I'll focus on land that falls within a major (or medium-size) city's "sphere of influence." This is land that is within the areas in a city's master plan for expansion. That means that essential services — roads and utilities, schools and emergency services — are targeted for these areas. (I will explain more about doing this research in Chapter Six.)

In short — you are looking for land within an identifiable path of growth.

Timing the cycles triggers the sale

SO HOW DO YOU determine the *right time* to buy a particular property to landbank?

Timing is even more important than *location*. This is because if the time is wrong, you cannot sell a parcel of dirt in even the most choice of locations. But if the time is right, you can even sell a parcel in a less-than-desirable location.

Timing boils down to the *economic cycle*. An economic cycle (also called a "business cycle") is the pattern of business activity, undulating like waves between the two extremes of boom and bust — of prosperity and recession. The traditional

---

[19] A building moratorium is a halt in the construction of homes or other structures. Governments may drastically limit the number of building permits, issued in an effort to slow or eliminate growth, due to such concerns as perceived overcrowding, inadequate water supply, insufficient infrastructure such as roads or sewer lines, or environmental harm allegedly caused by construction.

pattern is for an economy to hit four phases in this order: expansion, prosperity, contraction and recession (or depression). Then the cycle starts over again (with a "recovery"). In the pattern, there will be:

1) *Expansion* in the number of jobs and in industrial productivity while interest rates remain low or fall, meaning loans are not hard to come by and there is heavy consumer spending. In the real estate market, there will be plenty of construction activity of houses and buildings.

2) *Prosperity*, with plenty of money floating around, but prices rising (inflation) because demand outstrips the product supply, and interest rates rising. (The Federal Reserve Board raises rates to control inflation in an attempt to keep the economic cycle from swinging too quickly.) The real estate market is booming. Homes, retail centers and office complexes can't be built fast enough.

3) *Contraction* of the economy as consumers decide prices are too high — which results in a drop in purchases, less profits for businesses, a decline in productivity, and job layoffs. This is the vicious part of the cycle. In the real estate market, construction slows, a seller's market becomes a buyer's market, new homes take longer to sell, and retail and office complexes experience rising vacancy rates.

4) *Recession*, with a poor job market, high unemployment and sharp declines in business activity and prices. Interest rates eventually begin to fall. In real estate, this is the darkness before the dawn.

(See illustration of the economic cycle, on Page 50)

How does an economic cycle relate to landbanking?

It should be clear that the optimal times to buy land is during a downturn (optimally at the bottom of a recession) or the beginning of an upturn (the expansion) of the economy, when prices are lowest. But the investor then has to be prepared to hold onto the land until the cycle reaches its peak (the prosperity phase). (It's like buying stocks: You try to buy low and sell high.)

Let me say that we're mostly concerned with a *regional* economy, not the national economy. This is because regional economies can be booming even while the overall national economy is lagging. Of course, if interest rates are in the high double digits (meaning it's difficult to borrow money) or if there is a national recession, then regions everywhere are affected. But typically, some parts of the nation enjoy boom times while others are in a bust phase. As a landbanking investor, you must be concerned not only with the national economy, but with the economy of the area in which you intend to buy land. For example, after the dot-com bubble burst in the San Francisco Bay area in 2000 and 2001, northern California's economy took a downturn. But at the same time, Southern California's economy was in an upturn after an extended downturn due in part to closure of military bases.

The trick is to buy in a market where the economy is set to recover and enter the expansion phase. For if you buy in an overly depressed area, chances are the economy may never recover sufficiently to turn your landbanked acreage into pay dirt, or may take a great long time before its economy expands. (Think of a mill town, in which the mill shuts down. Or think of a mining town where the mine plays out or the price of the mineral being excavated falls on the world market, rendering the mine unprofitable.)

Therefore, the best bet seems to be buying in a real estate market that is due to expand imminently, or is beginning to expand already. This gets back to my point earlier in the chapter about zeroing in on a medium-size community with an increasing population, within commuting distance to a major city, with buildable land, a secure and proven water supply and a local government that encourages growth.

To repeat a point from earlier in the chapter: You want to buy land when urban sprawl is destined to reach the location within three to 10 years.

Target growing towns with eggs in many baskets

A FINAL POINT ABOUT growing real estate markets. Some areas are prone to boom and bust cycles. Often, their fortunes are tied to a single chief industry. These areas experience sharp increases in population and heavy home and land sales, followed by too much product on the market and sharp declines. Other areas are slow, steady growers. They sustain small but healthy population increases (for example, 2 percent a year) over a lengthy period (such as a decade or more). Their economies are diversified.

Precise timing is critical to investing in the boom-and-bust communities. Timing is less critical in the slow, steady markets.

ASSESSING A LOCAL ECONOMY

I gauge what phase a local economic cycle is in by its population increase over a period of time (say, 10 years); by the number of building permits issued each year; by the prices rising or falling on the real estate market; and by other economic data such as employment rates.

People don't move to an area because developers build houses. People move to an area for economic opportunity, and the developers supply them with homes.

How to gauge the data:

• A local government often keeps records of population in its jurisdiction on a year-to-year basis. Call and be directed to the right department from which to receive the data. (Or check the government's website.)

• A local government, usually its building department, will have records on the number of building permits issued per year. You often can get this data on-line.

• Contact the local board of Realtors to obtain figures on median home prices and average days on the market for homes to sell, and compare the figures by month and year.

• A state usually has a department, such as Research and Analysis, that records employment rates for specific communities in that state.

ASSESSING THE NATIONAL ECONOMY

I gauge what phase the national economic cycle is in by the abundance of "loose money." Toward the bottom of a cycle (as it contracts and heads into recession), only developers and builders with plenty of assets can borrow for projects, because the supply is tight. As a new cycle approaches its top (as prosperity nears its climax), banks and other lenders are willing to loan to any Tom, Dick or Harry who meets minimal criteria and has an investment in the works. Lenders figure the market is strong, and loaning to investors is smart.

This was the case in Nevada as I was writing these words in summer 2005. Money was very loose. A friend of mine's mother-in-law, who knew virtually nothing about real estate, was talking about buying rental properties, and arranging for business loans. Lenders considered her expert enough to lend to. The reality of such loose money floating around was a red flag for me. It indicated we were about at the top of the economic cycle, with a downturn ahead. It would not be an optimal time to buy, for land prices would be inflated.

I realized that the shoestring and speculative investors would end up paying too much for properties, and then the values would decline and they'd be forced to sell — only they'd now be competing with each other to sell, and prices would plummet further. (Lenders would foreclose on properties, too.) As the market cooled, opportunities for more circumspect investors would open up.

If possible, you want to buy at the bottom of a down cycle. When you do buy, your task will be to exercise patience, holding onto the property through the down cycles and into the up cycles until the price reaches a peak in. (Selling your property will be discussed more in Chapter Ten, in Part III.)

As I mentioned in the introduction and will again in Chapter Six, landbanking may not be for investors whose timetables don't allow them to wait five, seven or 10 years before selling and realizing a profit. But landbanking is a prime opportunity for investors who are at least 10 years from retirement.

GETTING 'SQUEEZED' BY A MEGALOPOLIS

Simply defined, a "megalopolis" is a very large urban complex, usually involving several cities or towns. It is a thickly populated "megapolitan" area that either is centered in a metropolis or embraces several metropolises.

Megapolitan areas are the reality of the present-day United States, and will only increase their populations, blurring the borders between traditional cities and towns, well into the 21st century. Researchers at 10 U.S. universities are examining the phenomenon with an eye on the future. A study at Virginia Tech predicted that 10 megapolitan areas, each with more than 10 million residents, will exist in the nation by 2040. The two largest megapolitan areas will be "Northeast," extending from Richmond, Virginia, north through Washington, D.C., Philadelphia, New York City and Boston (an area already home to 50.4 million people); and "Southland" — comprising Los Angeles, San Diego, Las Vegas and their suburbs (already home to 22.2 million people). Three smaller megapolitan areas will be "Valley of the Sun" (Phoenix to Tucson); "Cascadia" (Seattle to Portland and Eugene, Oregon); and "Norcal" (San Francisco to Sacramento).

The Cooleys, authors of the 1960s classic *The Simple Truth about Western Land Investment*, envisioned this demographic trend of a chief city and its suburbs both radiating out from the chief city's civic center and growing together, thanks to improved roads and population increases, to form "one great strip city." The Cooleys came up with their own word for "megalopolis": "megaloctopus," and added: "The forces which are causing these great conglomerate communities to reach out, and the directions in which they are certain to grow, are the two magic keys to future fortunes in real estate."

The Cooleys said the key to profiting from landbanking in the path of urban growth is "to get squeezed by a Megaloctupus; the trick is to be there when the bean and the potato fields are cut up into industrial parcels and the city lots and the light industries and rows of nearly identical tract houses are built." Quick on the heels of these developments will be a shopping center, around which will grow another complex of service businesses. The community's evolution into a functioning, incorporated city will be inevitable.

The Cooleys summarized that evolutionary pattern as "raw to agricultural to industrial to adjacent residential with a shopping and service complex located in the areas designated by the subdividers as C-zoned or commercially zoned property."

The pattern — obviously — is being repeated incessantly around the nation. University of Pennsylvania researchers foresee more than 300 million Americans (about 70 percent of the population) living in eight "super city" regions by 2050. If that is the case, then landbankers in the century's first decade shouldn't have too much trouble figuring out where the tentacles of megaloctopuses are stretching.

KEY POINTS TO REMEMBER:

☛ *Location* and *timing* are the factors that largely determine which properties should be considered as investments.

☛ A key to finding a prime property is a projection that urban sprawl will reach the area in three to 10 years, yet developers have yet to snatch up the property.

☛ "Urban sprawl" has a negative connotation, but can be thought of as a natural demographic phenomenon resulting from population growth and consumers' pursuit of quality of life. A simple definition from *Webster's*: "The spreading of urban developments (as houses and shopping centers) on undeveloped land near a city."

☛ To the landbanker's advantage, land developers compete fiercely for affordable land in growing markets, since land is the big cost variable to developers — construction and labor costs being fairly equal.

- Narrow your market search to growing, medium-size "bedroom communities" where homes can be built.
- Focus on undeveloped land within a city's "sphere of influence."
- *Timing* is even more important than *location*, and boils down to economic cycles. The goal is to buy at the bottom of a cycle and sell at its peak.
- An economic cycle, also called a business cycle, traditionally has four phases: expansion, prosperity, contraction and recession/depression.

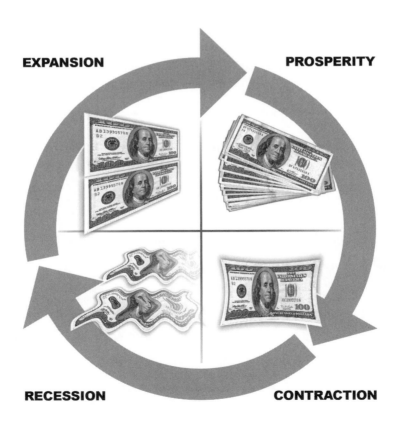

Researching a property can begin at home. Next stop: the local government.
If the parcel seems right, visit the site!

CHAPTER SIX

More Fundamentals of Landbanking

There are different ways of searching for potential properties for investment landbanking. There are, of course, the advertisements in magazines and newspapers, or promotional fliers that wind up in your mailbox, or infomercials on television or spam in your email inbox. There are tips from real estate agents or friends, acquaintances or neighbors, relatives or the guy you talked to at a cocktail party. (Just like tips on stock.)

What I like to do is follow up on leads from associates, or search through published articles or on the Internet, and focus on medium-size cities (as mentioned in Chapter Five) that are experiencing rapid growth. By "rapid growth," I'm referring to sheer population numbers, not a *rate* of growth, since a small town can increase by a few hundred people and have a high growth rate, while a large city can add tens of thousands of people but still have a small growth rate.

Next, I'll zero in on properties that fall within a city's sphere of influence (as mentioned in Chapter Five). Again, a "sphere of influence" is the areas listed in a city's master plan targeted for annexation by the city. The annexing will occur when warranted by each area's growth in tax base, which is tied to development. (My goal is to buy just before the builders show up looking for land on the market. I don't want to be competing with homebuilders or development companies for pieces of earth. I want to stay just ahead of them in distance in the path of growth. I try to buy properties five to seven years out of growth reaching the property.)

Zeroing in on properties within a growing medium-size city's sphere of influence will greatly narrow down my search. There are good investment properties all over our country, but you can't look at all of them. You must manage your time well, since you will need all the time you can muster to adequately research a specific property — perform due diligence — once you've found one in which you're strongly interested. (We'll discuss the matter of "due diligence" further down in this chapter.)

Two things to keep in mind while you cast about for potential investments worthy of your time and money:

1) There are many reasons why a seller has a piece of property on the market; therefore, there are good deals to be had. An investor may have bought a property 20 years before and seen its value increase significantly, and is ready to sell because a sale will fit into that investor's timetable. (For example, the investor may want the income for retirement.) Or maybe the owner inherited the property from a relative, and wants to realize cash instead of managing the investment. Or maybe the owner is experiencing financial difficulties and wants to liquidate the property.

2) You must resist being too hasty or impulsive in settling on a candidate for purchase. Opportunity does not knock only once.

My father is fond of saying that choosing the right investment is like being up at the plate in a baseball game — except that there is no umpire calling balls and strikes as the pitches come in. You can stand there, bat poised, as long as you want, waiting for just the right pitch to swing at. You can let as many go by as you care to. Some may look pretty good, but may not be right down the center of the plate. So you wait for one that is just perfect.

This analogy is pertinent to landbanking. There is a universe of deals out there, and new ones coming on the market every day. So be patient. Be picky. And be vigilant. Dismiss all the offerings outside your strike zone, but study each good-looking pitch carefully. Know that when that juicy meatball finally comes, you'll be making your home run swing.

54

What constitutes a home run ball?

What ingredients have to be in place for a profitable turnaround in a reasonable span of time (say, three to 10 years)?

Following are the proven ingredients from my experience and that of my mentors and partners. The more of the following ingredients in place, the shorter your hold time will be on a landbanked piece of property:

- The property is, at the minimum, fairly priced on the market. (You can determine this by comparing prices for comparable properties — "comps" — on the market.)

- The property is within eyeshot of new buildings (either recently built or being built) — schools, churches, fire stations, retail businesses. (A strong indicator that the property is within the path of growth.)

- The property falls within a fast-growing city's sphere of influence.

- The property is within serviceable, functional, practical distance from existing power, water and sewer lines. In other words, the property is within a utility's service area, there are existing facilities close enough to service the property, and the utility can feasibly extend the services to the property without a developer spending too much money for the extension.

A piece of land may seem to have all the virtues necessary to be a good investment, but something could still be amiss, such as a neighbor with a junkyard, or natural springs in the middle of the property. Take time to explore the vicinity.

- The property's size will be attractive to a developer in the not-too-distant future.
- The property's zoning will be attractive to a developer in the not-too-distant future.
- You can afford to buy the property and can financially carry it until it's sold. This includes paying the sales price and interest payments to the lender, and paying property taxes and other expenses of maintaining the property until it can be sold. (We'll cover these points in chapters Seven and Eight.)

With the exception of that last bullet point, determining whether a property is a home run ball — a sound investment — comes down to performing *due diligence*.

Due diligence from a distance, and on the spot

I'VE MENTIONED "DUE DILIGENCE" a number of times already in the preceding chapters. Performing due diligence just means doing a thorough study of a property to ensure it's a sound investment.

My method is to do as much research as possible on the Internet first, before ever visiting a property. This, of course, will save me time by helping me weed out properties that don't look like winners, or that could be marginal bets.

- I'll get a copy of the real estate broker's listing of the property — including the price and the property's various features. Realize, though, that the information in a broker's listing may not be accurate.
- I'll use a search engine to see what news articles say about the property's general area: weather, environment, economy, infrastructure, crime, and other major topics.
- I'll see what development is going into the area — both residential and commercial. (For example, is a Wal-Mart planned?)
- I'll look for the website of a real estate broker in the area that may contain the Multiple Listing Service ("MLS") for real estate, and look at the sales prices and days on the market ("DOM") of local properties comparable to the one I'm interested in.

If my Web research sustains my interest in the property, I'll contact a title company or seller's agent and request a *property report*. As mentioned in Chapter Four, this report contains crucial information such as the property's ownership, sales history, legal description, assessed tax value, size in square feet or acreage, and zoning.[20]

If the property is within a planned subdivision, I'll find if the state has issued a public report on the subdivision. The report would contain any warnings from the

---

[20] Experienced real estate investors who have forged relationships with title companies can often simply request a property report free of charge from a title company. Sometimes the investor will receive direct access to the title company's database.

local city or county government.

As mentioned in Chapter Four, if the property is part of a developer's subdivision, I'll research whether the developer has any consumer complaints on file by calling the office of the state attorney general, the area's Better Business Bureau, the U.S. Department of Housing and Urban Development, and the state's department of real estate.

If I'm still strongly interested in a property's potential at this point, I'll go out and visit it. While there, I may also poke around in the newspaper files of the local library, or even local newspaper of record, if public access is granted to its archives. (When I'm seriously interested in a particular area, I'll even subscribe to the local newspaper of record.)

I'll pay a visit to the local city or county planning department. The staffs know what development is happening or planned for in the area. They can provide the regional master plan and zoning maps, and information on zoning changes in the works or planned. They may even be able to provide information on the location of utilities, or direct you to the utility companies to receive that information. (Just remember, as always, to allow yourself enough time to get this information. You have to work within a staff's schedule and department hours.)

Since I'm in the landbanking business, I've worked with a lot of brokers. Sometimes I'll save myself the legwork of going around to government offices and utilities by asking the real estate broker — if he or she stands to earn a commission from a sale — to get me the information I need on zoning, planning and utilities.

A piece of dirt may seem to have all the virtues necessary to be a good investment, but something could still go wrong. Maybe the owner of a nearby lot has 53 junker cars parked on it and there is no county ordinance that says he can't have his private junkyard. Or maybe a neighbor has a pit bull puppy mill. Or maybe there are natural springs right in the middle of the property you've bought, and you can't build on it.

So I'll give myself enough time to explore the vicinity of a property. This is my opportunity to dig deeply into the worthiness of a property — to perform as thorough a reconnaissance as possible. To poke around and see what I can find.

Not long ago I looked at a piece of property that could be subdivided into three lots for single-family houses. Only a few lots away, a local builder was busy putting up homes. He already had built four or fives houses in this very area. A red flag (one of the eight classic ones mentioned in Chapter Four) unfurled in my mind: Why wasn't this builder — who was from the area, and making money in the area — buying the empty lots I was looking at?

It didn't add up. So I backed off. I came to find out the lots were over-priced.

Digging deeply below the surface

IF MY INTEREST CONTINUES to burn bright at this point of performing my due diligence, I'll take these two steps:

1) Contact a local title company and ask for a preliminary title report. This contains even more details on a property.[21]

2) Hire a real estate appraiser and have the property appraised. The appraiser will cost a bit of money (say, $750), but may come up with a figure significantly less than the asking sales price. (The figure may be less, too, than the comparable prices ("comps") that a real estate agent provides for the market.) The appraiser's figure can be a strong negotiating tool for the buyer.[22] An alternative

[21] If you do go forward and make a sales offer on a property, and it goes into escrow, you'll need to hire the services of a title company. The title company will check records to ensure the seller is the legal owner and there are no liens or other outstanding claims on the property and what easements, if any, are on the property. A preliminary title report, given by a title company, proves the seller is the rightful owner and lists any debtor claims against the property. (You want to be negotiating with the decision-maker, who is usually the owner, not someone else such as a relative. Also, if you discover the owner is delinquent in property taxes, it may place you in a stronger negotiating position.) The title company also sells title insurance. The buyer purchases an owner's policy protecting against loss stemming from ownership disputes.

[22] You may hire an appraiser even before visiting a property. If I've done my Web research and am strongly interested in a property, I may hire a local appraiser to not only give me a valuation of the property but to research where the utilities are in relation to the property, and the property's zoning. This means I will invest money in my search without having yet seen the property, but this step could save me a great deal of time, trouble and money by sparing me a trip out if the appraiser's information quashes the deal in my mind. On the downside, an appraiser's report can take several weeks to arrive, so you must gauge whether that could jeopardize your ability to land a good deal. If you hire an appraiser after making a sales offer, make sure you account for the time it will take to receive your appraisal report when determining the length of your due-diligence period.

to hiring an appraiser is obtaining a broker's price opinion ("BPO"), which is given by a real estate broker, sometimes free as a courtesy — since the broker will expect your business. However, a BPO is not as thorough, and possibly not as accurate, as an appraiser's report.

Finally, if I'm still strongly interested in a property but want to eliminate any remaining questions or possible red flags in my mind, I'll contact (and possibly hire the services of) additional experts. Here are some who may be appropriate:

- **Civil engineer.** Civil engineers are involved in every bit of land development that happens. They are the facilitators who take a piece of land through governmental approval processes, and design the streets, curbs and gutters, sewer, water and power lines. You can find civil engineers in the Yellow Pages under "Engineers." Call around. Find out their rates. Be willing to pay them for their time and expertise. Usually they charge by the hour. It's time well spent.

Civil engineers are qualified to give professional opinions on whether a property is buildable. Is the grade sufficient, or too steep? Are there environmental concerns? How much will it cost to bring in water? Is another developer already bringing water and other utilities close to your property (which could raise your property's value)? And so on.

Civil engineers who've worked in a geographic area for a period of time know what's going on with development and construction in that area. I once looked at a property near a small California town. My partners and I hired a civil engineer, who alerted us to a newspaper article about environmental concerns related to a nearby asbestos mine. Our real estate agent had forgotten to tell us about that.

- **Soil engineer.** An expert must analyze the soil to determine whether it can support a lawn and garden, whether the soil would make it problematic for land development (such as expansive clays and rock), and whether there's any other serious problem. For example, if the property contains fill, there could be a possibility of sinkage. In fact, if there's any question that the soil may pose a serious issue — perhaps it appears rocky, or there was mining or industrial operations nearby that may have polluted it, or there could be natural springs underneath — a soil engineer can tell you.

My father the homebuilder bought a large piece of property one time, planning to develop it as a subdivision. He ended up not making as much money as expected on the investment, because just beneath the surface of the soil were thousands of river rocks the approximate size of cantaloupes. They were strewn across the property — tons of them. The cost of pulling them out, stacking them up and having them hauled away was tremendous. When my father bought the property, he saw some flat rocks poking out here and there, never suspecting the tapioca pudding of stones he'd have to deal with.

If only he'd hired a soil engineer to check out the property first!

- **Local developer.** Not too long ago a broker showed me five residential lots zoned for duplexes on a street that had 20 residential lots. The five lots, whose owner was a woman who'd had them about 15 years, appeared good to me. The street had been paved. There were utilities in the area. A fire station was around the corner and backed up to one of the lots. The only big question in my mind was why all 20 lots on the street remained vacant. Why hadn't a builder come in?

I found a local developer and asked what he knew about the 20 lots. "Let me tell you," he said, "I don't think they'll perc."

By "perc" he meant "percolate," as in passing a percolation test. A percolation test is performed on a lot's soil to determine whether it can hold a septic tank (which is necessary when a property doesn't tie into a sewer line).

My next call was to a local septic-tank company, and through that connection I was put in touch with a soil engineer who did percolation tests. I explained to him my concerns. He immediately recognized the lots and confirmed that they wouldn't perc.

The lots were worthless until a sewer line was extended to them. And it could take decades for the local government to create a sewer district and for the utility to construct a sewer plant and extend the line. I called the real estate broker and said I was going to pass.

I saw that another property on the street was for sale, by a different broker.

Out of curiosity, I called this broker and asked the price for the lot. Then I asked if there were any problems with the lot. One of my questions was, "Any problems with septic?"

"We don't know," the broker said. "Do your own due diligence."

His response smelled like verbal sewage. It was a bright red flag to me!

If I were selling a piece of property, I'd want to gather as complete information as possible about it. This extra information could interest a buyer over all the other properties competing with it on the market. I'd provide all the pertinent facts — including "sewer's here, water's there, power's right over here." I'd provide thorough information for their due diligence.

The broker was obviously stonewalling. I was more than happy to walk away from that street.

Tying up the property in escrow

A SPECIAL NOTE MUST be inserted at this point. *Due diligence takes time.* But you DON'T want to lose out on buying a piece of property that looks good by having another buyer beat you to the sale while you're still researching.

How to prevent this?

One way to protect your interest in a promising property is to get the deal into escrow right away. If you think the property could be a winner, but there is still due diligence to perform, make a purchase offer contingent on

---

To prevent losing out on a promising property while continuing your due diligence, get the deal into escrow.

---

completion of a due-diligence period. If the offer is accepted, you pay the small fee to an escrow company (say, $500, and make it refundable to you if the deal doesn't close). Then *you* control the sale until the due-diligence period ends (for example, after 45 days). You set the due-diligence period with the seller, and also set the close-of-escrow period. (For example, the close-of-escrow could be 60 days from the time the property enters escrow, or 15 days after the 45-day due-diligence period ends.)

Due diligence equals peace of mind

THE BENEFITS OF COMPLETING thorough due diligence are threefold:

1) You've eliminated investing in a property of dubious merit.
2) You've increased your knowledge of real estate in general.
3) You can sleep easier at night, knowing you've done everything in your power to research a good investment.

Due Diligence Checklist

After zeroing in on a worthy market in which to invest, and finding a promising property:

✔ Get a copy of a real estate broker's listing for the property.

✔ Get a property report. Verify the property's exact size. Determine who the owner is. Compare prices for other properties in the neighborhood. Review the property's assessed value and previous purchase price.

✔ Verify zoning, specifically whether the lot can be developed as is, and what can be built on it.

✔ Locate the area's utility providers and determine the cost of servicing the property with water, power and sewer.

✔ Obtain engineer's reports, if desired, on the buildability of the property and any environmental concerns.

KEY POINTS TO REMEMBER:

☞ Good investment properties can be found all over the country, and the landbanker can't consider every one. A way to zero in on prospects is to follow up on leads from associates, or to search through printed articles or on the Internet for growing bedroom communities and look for undeveloped land for sale within a city's sphere of influence.

☞ Two points to consider when analyzing a piece of property:

1) There are many reasons why a seller is selling — such as liquidating an inheritance, or weathering a personal financial crisis — so good deals can be found.

2) Because good deals can be found, resist being too hasty in grabbing any particular deal.

☞ Seven ingredients needed for a profitable, timely turnaround:

1) The property is fairly priced when you buy it.

2) The property is within eyeshot of new buildings.

3) The property falls within a fast-growing city's sphere of influence.

4) The property is near to power, water and sewer lines. In other words, the property is within a utility's service area.

5) The property is large enough to interest a developer.

6) The zoning will interest a developer.

7) You can afford to carry the property until it's sold.

☞ There are three phases to performing due diligence — from a distance; in the actual area; at the site using experts.

☞ Six parts of performing due diligence from a distance:

1) Use an Internet search engine and find what news articles say in general about a property's area.

2) See what development is planned or going into an area.

3) Review a real estate agent's Multiple Listing Service from the area. (This often can be done on-line.)

4) Request a property report from the title company.

5) If the property is within a planned subdivision, check if the state has issued a public report on the subdivision, and if the report contains any warnings by the local government.

6) If the property is part of a developer's subdivision, check whether any complaints against the developer are on file.

☛ Three parts of performing due diligence in the area:

1) Review articles and information at the local newspaper or library.

2) Visit the local government's planning department and review the regional master plan, zoning maps and information on the location of utilities.

3) Visit the site and its immediate vicinity, looking for red flags.

☛ Three parts of performing due diligence at the site:

1) Obtain a preliminary title report from a title company.

2) Have a real estate appraiser appraise the property. (Or get a broker's price opinion — "BPO.")

3) Have experts evaluate the property. Experts can include a civil engineer, a soil engineer and a developer.

☛ Due diligence takes time, so getting a property into escrow can prevent losing the deal to another investor.

The larger the value of the investment, the greater the leverage for the investor.

CHAPTER SEVEN

Leverage

Leverage: The use of borrowed money or credit to enhance one's speculative capacity for profit.

The point is made in popular how-to books on buying rental properties that the way for a small investor to get into a $1 million home is to put up 10 percent ($100,000) and borrow $900,000 from a bank. The power of this strategy is that the investor will enjoy all the profits from the appreciation in value of the $1 million property while the bank (or other lending institution) will simply earn the interest off the principal of the loan.

If the property goes up, say, 12 percent in value (a gain of $120,000), the small investor can sell the property, pay off the $900,000 plus the interest (say it's 6 percent — or $54,000) and realize a profit of $66,000. That's a staggering 66 percent return on the $100,000 investment.[23]

Contrast that with a different scenario: The small investor instead invests the $100,000 into stocks. Earning 12 percent on them would yield him $12,000.

By leveraging his $100,000 with a $900,000 bank loan (a debt-equity ratio of 9:1) at a normal (as of this writing) loan interest rate of 6 percent in the real estate market, the small investor earns 5½ times more than what he could have in the stock market. What's more, banks and other lending institutions don't make

---

[23] This, of course, is a very generalized example, not taking into account fees to purchase and sell the house, expenses of maintaining it, mortgage payments or income from rent. In all likelihood, the return on the investment will be even higher than 66 percent, since rental income may exceed all other expenses and yield a net profit itself. There also will be tax issues.

loans for stock purchases. They do, however, make loans on something tangible and historically valuable: real estate.

The above example about the power of leverage concerned rental properties. This book is concerned with investing in pre-development land. Good land is attractive to lenders, and lenders include more than banks. Landowners, themselves, can finance buyers to purchase the land. Maybe a landowner is tired of carrying the land, paying the property taxes and insurance. He finances a buyer's purchase. Worst-case scenario if the buyer defaults on payments? The landowner forecloses on the land.

Good raw land in the path of development can often be financed by a bank loan for between 30 to 50 percent of the purchase price ("loan to value").[24] But if the property is out a ways from current construction activity — say, it looks to be another five years or more before developers will be interested in it — a savvy buyer often can get the *seller* to finance 80 to 90 percent of the purchase. That's why seller financing is standard in the land-investment market.[25]

This way of thinking is foreign to many small investors. They think all they have to invest is the money that sits in their savings account. They are intimidated by the large figures of purchase prices. All those zeros![26]

But all an investor should be focused on is raising the 10 to 20 percent of the purchase price to get into the deal. If the deal is a good one — intelligently researched and chosen, with the interest payments and other expenses affordable to the investor, and pays off as it should — then the power of leverage will reward the investor many times over.

---

[24] The reason banks don't lend as much for land investments as for house or building investments is because land is less liquid than physical structures. The market of buyers for homes and buildings is much larger. Buyers of empty land, in contrast, are either developers, landbankers or investors (and, occasionally, governmental agencies or land conservancies who want to preserve the land as vacant). As I wrote these words, many banks were lending 30 percent for undeveloped land at a relative distance from a city's growth but up to 50 percent for land ready to build with utilities already in place and in or close to a city. The annual interest rate, by the way, on a loan on vacant land was 12 percent — much higher than the rate on loan-to-value or on property with physical structures on it, such as rental homes.

[25] There are some lenders, often community banks, who will loan on improved property — for example, residential lots in platted subdivisions that already have streets and utilities ("curb, gutter, water, sewer") put in, and are ready to be built on. But on a raw, unimproved piece of land, you are pretty much limited to four financing options other than footing the entire bill yourself: 1) a loan from a bank for 30 to 50 percent of the purchase price; 2) financing through the seller; 3) finding partners and paying in cash; 4) finding a private (non-bank)

If the timing is right, leveraging is especially lucrative

NOT LONG AGO AS I wrote these words, a friend of mine bought a piece of land in Southern California for $150,000. She put $50,000 down out of her own pocket, and invested another $50,000 to engineer the property (getting governmental

---

The investor should focus on raising the 10 to 20 percent of the purchase price. The power of leverage will reward the investor many times over in a good investment.

---

approvals — "entitlements" — to have it zoned for development) to make it more attractive to a developer. The value of the property has appreciated enormously. The value as of this writing was $1.8 million. Consider her profit were my friend to sell it for this price. There was her out-of-pocket investment of $100,000, plus paying off the $100,000 loan and its 8 percent interest ($8,000), and 10 percent in broker's fees ($180,000). Her profit would be $1,412,000. Not a bad return, huh?

Again, the power of leverage.

As a side note about the aforementioned deal — the people my friend bought the property from had held onto it for eight years, and were disappointed it hadn't appreciated greatly in value. From my friend's due diligence, she saw that the property was ripe to soar in value. Her offer to the owners was the first they'd received — and to my friend's benefit, they took it. Had they held onto the

---

lender, usually an individual investor, who likely will charge a stiffer interest rate than would a bank. Let's examine one more option: Having the seller carry the financing, but also getting a loan from a bank. As an example of this scenario, the seller may agree to finance most of the purchase, but insist that the buyer pay a large down payment. If, say, the entire price for the property is $200,000 and the down payment is 30 percent ($60,000), the buyer can ask a bank to finance that. The bank will agree — but only by being in the "first position" for ownership of the lot if the borrower (the buyer of the property) becomes delinquent in payments on the bank loan. That means that the seller will be in the "second position," and if the buyer defaults, then the bank takes over the property and the seller will have to pay off the balance of the buyer's $60,000 loan before recouping the property. Not surprisingly, sellers are not as likely to agree to this type of financing arrangement than a straightforward purchase by the buyer with the seller remaining in first position.

[26] Ironically, a homeowner is, in effect, leveraging his down payment on his home when he takes out a mortgage to complete the purchase. If the home appreciates appropriately in value, the rate of return can be very handsome. But many homeowners don't consider buying a home with a mortgage as an investment.

property for another 18 months and not grown anxious, they would have been rewarded handsomely.

This is why timing (as explained in Chapter Five) is critical to a successful investment. This point will be explored in greater depth in Chapter Ten.

Find the deal, then find the money

AFTER NEARLY TWO DECADES and numerous investments in real estate, I can't emphasize enough that the right mentality for success involves first finding the property. If you ferret out a great piece of land to invest in, that's when you start considering how to finance the purchase.

First, find the deal that's worthwhile. Then go hunt for the money.

Of course, you don't want to lose out on the deal while you put your financing together. So what you do is tie it up into escrow for a set period of time — which would include the time to perform due diligence (as explained in Chapter Six). The cost for putting the deal into escrow may cost a few thousand dollars, but can be fully refundable to you if the deal cancels. Now *you* are in control.

First find the right property, then hunt for the money to buy it.

Of course, I am an experienced landbank investor with a strong track record for successful investments. I have many business connections. Therefore, my options for financing are more numerous than that of a newer investor. So my best advice to someone just starting out is to seek a deal that is seller financed. You won't need to qualify for a loan from a bank, submitting lots of paperwork on your financial situation. Through seller financing you can usually get a reasonable interest rate (perhaps 2 points higher than what a bank would charge for a home mortgage at current rates — although you should start your negotiation at as low a rate as possible as you see advertised in newspapers or on-line). If the seller will carry 80 to 90 percent of the purchase price, you will be operating on a debt-to-equity ratio of 4:1 or 9:1.

To repeat a previously made point: Your capacity for profit will be much greater than if you were to invest your equity by itself in, say, stocks or bonds, yielding a rate of return solely on the equity — instead of enjoying a rate of return on a far greater sum leveraged by the equity.

Another way to finance an investment

THERE IS ANOTHER WAY to finance an investment property other than approaching a lending institution or private lender, or asking the seller to make the loan. This way of leveraging involves working with fellow investors either in partnerships or in special corporate entities.

We'll explore that in Chapter Eight.

FINDING THE SELLER'S 'HOT BUTTON'

So often, the needs of the seller shape the sale. If a seller receives multiple offers on the property, the buyer whose offer best meets the desires of the seller will prevail. And this doesn't always mean the highest offer.

When I buy a property, I try to find out what the seller's "hot button" is. I'll politely ask questions. "What interests you most from selling this property? Are you looking for a cash out, or are you looking for monthly income?" Maybe the seller is retired and living on a fixed income, and wants to augment that with a monthly check from selling the property. Or maybe the seller is looking to liquidate the property to invest it elsewhere. In this latter case, I might explain that the interest rate I'm willing to pay, if the seller carries me on the loan, would be higher than what the seller would get in the stock or bond market.

Hot buttons vary with each seller. For example, when I was negotiating with the owner of a parcel in Southern California, I learned that he wanted to sell the

Every seller has a "hot button." The diligent buyer needs to press the right one.

property and be done with it. He explained that he'd already had to take it back from a previous buyer who'd defaulted on payments. It had been a major hassle and the owner didn't want to deal with that situation again.

I was able to show him that my financials were sound and my track record of investing was solid. So I was able to get into the property for a relatively low down payment and the low interest rate of 5 percent.

KEY POINTS TO REMEMBER:

- The power of leveraging an investment comes from the return based on the *entire value* of the property, which is proportionally higher than what the return would be based only on the investor's equity.

- Banks typically offer financing on 30 to 50 percent of the purchase price ("loan to value") of raw land in the path of development. Therefore, an investor must find additional financing or come up with a large down payment.

- A savvy investor often can get the seller to finance 80 to 90 percent of the purchase. Seller financing is standard in the land-investment market. Interest rates on seller financing are negotiable, but expect to pay a couple points higher than the going rate at banks for a home mortgage.

- A wise strategy is focusing first on finding a great piece of land, then working on coming up with the financing.

- When negotiating a purchase, it's useful to politely ask questions to find out the seller's "hot button" — what the seller wants most from the sale. Is it a cash out? Is it a monthly check? Is it assuredness that you, the buyer, can afford the property and the seller won't have to foreclose on it? Then work to meet the seller's needs, and negotiate favorable terms for yourself (such as a low interest rate on seller financing) in exchange.

Be selective whom you choose as partners. The grief you'll save will be your own.

CHAPTER EIGHT

Groups and Partners

Another way to finance a property purchase and leverage an investment is to partner with another investor or put together a team of investors who pool their money. If done correctly, the results can be extremely rewarding.

In fact, this method is precisely what my company — Land Resource Investments, Inc. — employs on a grand scale. LRI assembles teams of small investors to raise capital to compete for valuable land against large corporations with plenty of purchasing power. It is our way of getting into a bigger game. As mentioned in this book's introduction, LRI was founded in 1999 after Richard Ramsey, my business associate at the time, began lobbying California's Department of Real Estate to permit the practice of a company selling a single parcel of land to multiple investors. In return, each of these investors would receive title to ownership in the land parcel in the form of a grant deed insured by a policy of title insurance. The Department of Real Estate approved the practice after great scrutiny and review.

This model has let small investors group together to buy the sort of valuable undeveloped real estate usually only available to the purchasing power of big investors. And from 2000 to the present, as I wrote these words, LRI has managed more than a dozen landbanking projects, involving thousands of investors, in California. LRI does the legwork — finding real estate with high potential in the path of urban growth, and performing due diligence on the property — then recruits investors. [27]

But let's talk about smaller projects for now.

If, on your own, you team up with one or more investors, you can buy property that you, as an individual investor, normally couldn't afford. That is the single biggest positive of joining others in an investment property. You will be able to leverage your investment.

Teaming up with one or more investors can let you buy property you normally couldn't afford and leverage your investment.

The biggest downside to such an arrangement is that you can lose control of managing the investment. Partners or groups, because two or more minds are involved, will almost assuredly have differing opinions on when to hold or sell the property. (From my experience, if you have 20 people in a room, you'll get 21 opinions! Imagine trying to form a consensus. What will form much quicker are factions.) This can complicate taking decisive action when decisive action is most needed — when timing the market and deciding to sell, and when approving or rejecting a specific purchase offer. Some partners will want to sell now; some will want to hold for the future. Some will want to take the first offer; others will want to be patient.

When money's involved, emotions can run high. Personality conflicts develop. Time and energy are burned up.

And there are other complications inherent in an investment involving two or more investors. One of the investors may be unable to make a monthly payment, leaving the other investor(s) to either cover the payment, buy out the delinquent investor's share, or seek a new investor to replace the delinquent one. Also, there are

---

[27] For more information on Land Resource Investments, Inc., visit the website: www.landbanknation.com. Information is also included in the section toward the end of the book, "About Land Resource Investments, Inc."

certain managerial tasks involved in owning a landbanked property. Someone has to be in charge of ensuring payments are collected and sent to the seller, property taxes are paid, and the land is kept up and posted with signs, or fenced if necessary, so that no health hazards or public nuisances occur (such as overgrown weeds, trash heaped on the property or vagrants camping on it). Of course, someone has to be in charge of receiving purchase offers, and advertising the property.

In other words, one of the investors must be the managing partner. This person must keep the other investors regularly informed about the status of the property and the market.

You can see now how being in a partnership or investment group can demand extra time and energy that would not need to be expended were you in the investment by yourself.

Some of my own small investments illustrate this point. For example, I own two adjacent lots in Southern California. One of the lots I own by myself; the other I own with a friend. He owns 40 percent of that lot — and therefore is a minority partner, while I'm the majority partner with 60 percent. That means I enjoy the power of decision-making. I can sell the lot when I believe it's ready to sell (although, out of professional courtesy as well as friendship, I would discuss the deal in advance with my partner). He'd found the deal and brought it to me, and we have a good relationship. Still, having a partner complicates issues and takes up time when I have to pay property taxes or installments to the seller. The payments have to be split up between him and me.

Here are two more brief examples from my personal experience:

1) I owned land one time with a partner, and planned to build houses on it. The partner insisted that the garages be oversized. Why? Because he wanted his home to have an oversized garage. But all of our homebuilding competitors in that market were building standard-size garages. That meant we'd have to charge more for our houses. We could price ourselves out of the market.

2) I was building a house on a piece of property I owned with a partner. He wanted the house to have pink kitchen tile. The color was kind of pretty, but I

preferred to put in tile that 98 percent of buyers would like: beige or white.

When differences usually arise in partnerships or group investments, it is when the subject of selling comes along. Imagine the heated debates among people of contrary ideas. The cliché is that the least seaworthy "ship" is a partnership. Relationships — including family bonds and friendships — can easily become strained when bickering or flat-out shouting erupts in a room over whether to accept a sales offer.[28]

For this reason, I personally will involve myself in only two kinds of partnerships:

1) One where I am in 100 percent control, as a managing partner with the power of making all the decisions — whether it's having weeds removed, collecting property-tax payments from investors, adding entitlements (such as rezoning, and dividing the property into smaller lots — which will be discussed in Chapter Nine), having the property listed for sale, accepting or rejecting a purchase offer, and so on. I want my partner(s) to put up (their money) and shut up. I'll have the partnership agreement specify how much money I can spend on various duties.[29]

2) One where I have 0 percent control — and just park my investment in the property, trusting that it will prove profitable under the direction of someone else. I need not spend time or energy on decision-making. I just put up and shut up. (This situation isn't easy for many investors to handle. They have to emotionally divorce themselves from managing the investment and just not worry about it.)

Legally partnering with people you know

IN THE EARLY PART of your career as a landbanking investor, you may

---

[28] One strategy for a group of investors in dealing with a solitary member who wants to sell while the rest don't is simply to buy out the interest of the solitary partner or find another investor to buy the partner out.

[29] To facilitate such an arrangement, you can have each partner sign a limited power of attorney authorizing you to legally act on behalf of the partnership. Before a property is actually sold, make sure the power of attorney is updated. Title companies don't like powers of attorney that are older than six months.

not have the option of being a majority partner. That's OK. Joining a partnership or investment group can still be a great option for you. You will be able to better leverage your investment than if you were to pursue a less expensive, less valuable and less salable piece of property on your own (larger parcels are more attractive to builders and developers than smaller ones, because they can build more homes or structures and make a larger profit). You also are bound to learn a great deal about landbanking.

A crucial qualification must be inserted here. If private individuals want to form investment partnerships or groups, the members must enjoy pre-existing relationships with each other. A pre-existing relationship can be a relative, neighbor, coworker, dentist, doctor or lawyer, and so on — people within an individual's sphere of influence.[30] Or more simply put: people you know. The U.S. Security and Exchange Commission forbids common investors from advertising for, or otherwise soliciting investments from, strangers. The SEC requires that real estate brokers seeking investors meet specific regulations. You can get licensed as a real estate broker to seek investors. But there are partnerships and groups you can form with people solely through the aforementioned pre-existing relationships.

Some legal forms of partnerships and groups[31]:

- **Limited partnership.** This entity requires at least one "general partner" — who is in charge of decision-making, and the only partner who can legally obligate the business — and at least one limited partner. An LP-1 form is filed with the state. The general partners are the only ones who can be held personally liable for debts of the partnership, while the limited partners are only liable to the extent of their investments. The general partners usually enjoy full managerial control. Although a partnership agreement and annual meeting

---

[30] "Sphere of influence" also refers to land that is designated in a city's master plan as an area in which the city will grow.

[31] In addition to the three corporate entities mentioned in this chapter, here are three other entities involving two or more investors: C Corporation, S Corporation, Limited Liability Company. With each of these entities, articles of incorporation must be filed with the secretary of state in the particular state in which the entity is incorporating. With the C and S corporations, bylaws and annual meetings are required. With LLCs, an operating agreement and annual meetings are not required, but are recommended. Each of these entities protects shareholders or members from personal liability for more information, go to www.corporatedirect.com.

are not required, such an agreement can specify that consent of all partners is required before transferring interests in the property (such as selling shares or the entire property). In most states, investors have an option to form a limited liability partnership (LLP) by which each partner is only liable for business debts of the company, and not for acts of wrongdoing by any of the other partners in the course of the partnership's business.

- **General partnership.** This entity requires at least two general partners. No form needs to be filed with the state, and no annual meeting or partnership agreement is required, but a partnership agreement is recommended. The agreement (which can be written or oral, but written is recommended) can require consent of all partners before transferring interests in the property. This entity involves unlimited liability of the partners — meaning each partner could be held personally liable for the entire amount of debts and actions (including negligence) of the partnership, including those incurred by any of the other partners on behalf of the partnership. Any partner can bind the partnership by entering into a contract on behalf of the partnership. This can make this form of entity dangerous.

- **Tenancy in common.** Don't be misled by the word "tenancy." The partners are owners, not tenants. In this arrangement, investors can divide up the percentages of ownership. For example, one may own 50 percent of the property, another 10 percent, another 8 percent, and so on. And none of the partners own designated parts of the property (such as one owning the southeast corner, another the frontage acreage). Each owner can deal independently with his or her portion — such as selling, mortgaging or gifting it. (Note: "Tenancy in common" is not to be confused with "joint tenancy," a form of ownership by two or more parties sharing equal rights and control of an entire property — such as in a marriage — with each partner having the right of survivorship if another partner dies.)

Professional legal advice will help you decide which ownership entity to select.

Choosing good partners, avoiding problematic partners

WHAT TO LOOK FOR in selecting partners? You are looking within your sphere of influence. People with whom you enjoy pre-existing relationships.

If you're the one shopping a project around, you'll want to believe 100 percent in the project. You'll want to be sure to have done your homework. You'll want to have the genuine attitude that you're doing other investors a favor by bringing the project to them. And the first question you should ask each potential partner is whether he or she is looking to make an investment. If the answer is yes, then the person will be obligated to listen to you.

Since you'll have performed thorough due diligence on the investment project, you'll have hard numbers to show — what the property's worth, why it's an attractive investment, how the financing will work. You'll have something in writing — a prospectus.[32] So when you say, "Hey, I've got a land deal and it could be a winner," you'll have the information to back yourself up and increase the

---

When pitching a project to potential partners, the more details you provide, the more interest you generate.

---

chance that the person's initial decision won't be to pass. The more details you can provide right away, the more interest you're likely to generate, and the less likely you'll waste your time and theirs in a futile quest for investors. (And when you land your first partner, this fact alone — that you have another investor on board — should help you recruit more partners. You can share that information with more prospects; also, each partner brought aboard may recruit peers.)

Now, if you're the one being approached to be a partner in an investment, by someone shopping around an investment, you'll want to check out the prospectus,

---

[32] A prospectus should contain a property profile from the title company, a preliminary title report listing the current owner, maps of the property, services and utilities in the area of the property, the partnership agreement (showing which type of entity will be used and how the partnership will be structured), investment exit strategies (a Plan A and a Plan B), an estimate of the property taxes, and estimates of other expenses (such as legal fees or weed removal).

see how the deal is structured — and whether the person approaching you has any of his or her own money in the deal, and how much. (That's called having "skin in the game.") If your interest is kindled by the presentation, you'll want to do enough of your own legwork to be certain in your mind that the information you've received is accurate, and that the investment looks to be a winner.

If I'm the one recruiting investors, three types of people whom I try to exclude are those who over research, those who are overly emotional, and those in financial situations who can't really afford to risk investment capital.

- Over-researchers are people who research projects to death without being able to commit themselves. It's as if they do research for research's sake. This sort of person will dig and dig, and dig some more into the information about a potential investment, and continually raise one objection after another. I call this "analysis paralysis."

Here is an example of an over-researcher. One gentleman who had expressed interest in investing in one of Land Resource Investments, Inc.'s, landbanking projects in California phoned me recently as I wrote these words. He'd attended two of LRI's seminars. The reason for his phone call was that a statement on one of LRI's fact sheets bothered him. The statement was that California's population would increase to between 42 million and 48 million by 2020.

"That's really not a fact," he said, "that's a projection."

Well, true, it *is* a projection. But it's based on hard numbers gathered by the U.S. Census Bureau, California Department of Finance, and the Public Policy Institute of California. In essence, the Golden State is annually experiencing 500,000 births a year against 200,000 deaths, plus 300,000 more immigrants than emigrants. That's 600,000 new residents each year. Analysis by experts shows the trends accounting for these increases will continue into 2020.

The over-researcher insisted that this piece of information be labeled a "projection," not a "fact."

My response: "Well, is it a fact the sun is going to rise tomorrow? It hasn't yet."

His answer: "No, it's not a fact."

More often than not, the investor with analysis paralysis will allow his/her interest in the project to wither away, or will see the opportunity vanish because another party has seized it. Maybe this was the over-researcher's subconscious intention all along — to justify not pursuing the investment. Maybe the motive was self-affirmation about how intelligent the person is, able to crunch numbers and consider a project from every angle. Or maybe the motive was to be reassured that his/her current investments (such as in the stock market) were sound and superior to shifting money into landbanking. In the final analysis, the unending research served to personally legitimize the over-researcher's lack of decision.

The only way I would enter a business venture with this sort of person is one

Avoid partnering with people prone to over research, who are overly emotional or who can't afford the financial risk. Seek partners who prudently research but commit when satisfied, are businesslike and can afford risk.

in which the over-researcher was in charge as the general partner, and I had zero decision-making. To the credit of the over-researcher mentioned above who was skeptical about the sun rising, he appeared to be a very successful stock-market investor. As he explained to me, he'd never lost money on a stock — although he'd had to hold onto some stocks longer than he'd liked until they panned out. Perhaps he should become a money manager.

- The overly emotional person is incapable of looking at an investment objectively and dispassionately. A cool head is required in business, and particularly so in real estate investing, when face-to-face negotiations occur among sellers, buyers and agents.

Here is an example of an overly emotional person. I co-own some property in Southern California with a partner. She has a minority percent share, meaning that I, as majority partner, have the power of decision-making. Still, to keep the business relationship strong, I involve my partner with all decisions.

When we were negotiating with the lot's seller over the purchase price, my partner could not maintain a poker face and even keel. (You don't want to show excitement, eagerness or disdain in a negotiation, for this gives ammunition to the other side. The other side can gauge the level of interest and adjust the sales price or offer accordingly. Better to leave the other side in doubt over whether you're prepared to simply walk away.) I made an initial offer; the seller exclaimed, "I'm not going to take that!" OK, I thought, let's see what his counteroffer is. But my partner got wound up over the seller's reaction and visibly took offense. This physical display showed the seller that we were strongly interested in the property. My partner's behavior could have driven up the price significantly. (Or, if the behavior rubbed the seller the wrong way, it could have scotched the deal.) As it happened, my partner's emotional exhibit prolonged the dickering.

An overly emotional person also can become attached to a property, as if it were a family pet. When the time comes to sell, this sort of person has a hard time letting go, not viewing the situation rationally.

- People who can't afford to risk investment capital can complicate or compromise a venture because they may be too worried about their money to allow an investment the time to mature. They may be too eager to sell. Therefore, I try to avoid partners whose money is not discretionary investment capital. There is risk in almost any kind of investment (municipal bonds, certificates of deposit, and bank savings accounts are among the very few exceptions, and they offer extremely low returns). You want your partners to be able to handle the worst-case scenario in which an entire investment is lost. Of course, you minimize that possibility through due diligence and competent management. But you also need partners willing and able to stay the course until an investment significantly increases in value to yield a good return. If one of the partners needs his or her "lunch money" back, it can influence the other partners to sell prematurely.

The people you want to partner with, therefore, are investors who are:

- Prudent in researching a property, but fully able to commit to the investment once they're reasonably satisfied of its good potential (I term this "the entrepreneurial spirit"). You don't want someone impulsive who will write a check without even looking at a property. After all, that sort of person could prove impulsive during the sales phase.

- Emotionally stable and businesslike — willing to walk away if the price isn't right, and willing to buy or sell when the price is right. This person will remain cool, calm and collected during negotiations, not tipping your side's hand.

- Able to sustain a loss in a worst-case scenario, but dedicated to seeing the investment through to profitable maturity.

Such investors can be worth their weight in gold. They are not easy to find.[33]

Partnering can lead to further ventures

A FINAL NOTE ABOUT partnerships and groups: Fellow investors can form long-term business relationships that can be beneficial for future investments. Each investor knows people within his or her sphere of influence, and this extended network can bring in new partners for more investments, and new leads on profitable ventures.

This is important. Pursuing a variety of land opportunities helps the investor diversify risk. Just as a savvy securities investor balances a portfolio among stocks in different industries and with companies of different sizes with growth or earnings potential, the landbanking investor diversifies holdings.

Imagine you have $100,000 to invest. Is it better to go it alone and buy a $100,000 property by yourself, putting all your eggs in one basket, or better to be into four different $100,000 deals for $25,000 apiece with partners?

---

[33] One category of investor that I've found good to work with is people who have ample assets yet aren't really aware of it. A perfect example is a person who's accumulated a sizable 401(k) as an employee, is a fair number of years from retirement, and has left the employer and is seeking to roll over the retirement account into an Individual Retirement Account. An IRA can be used for real estate investing. This investor is not going to be anxious for the investment to mature quickly, since the funds are regarded as a long-term investment not meant to reach maturity and be drawn upon until retirement age.

In the last analysis, if you can afford to go it alone, with sufficient capital to invest and enough time and know-how to ferret out promising properties, then don't take on partners. You will avoid the potential politics and time-consuming decision-making. But if you're starting out, and can't afford to go it alone, partnering with other investors can make all the sense in the world. Especially if there are experienced, successful investors in the group. In contrast, inexperienced investors can doom a partnership from the start.

While writing this chapter, I was in the process of purchasing 40 acres from an older woman in California who'd owned and sold a great many properties in her real estate career. I was buying the land from her at what I was satisfied was a good price. While my deal was a good one, I was aware that the seller — we'll call her Amanda — had taken advantage of other buyers in the past.

The least seaworthy ship is a partnership.

One of these buyers was a woman I know. We'll call her Jeanette. Jeanette had bought 10 acres from Amanda a decade earlier. Jeanette couldn't really afford to make payments on the property by herself. So Amanda had facilitated the sale by assembling a team of buyers that included Jeanette plus three other investors.

Unfortunately, the 10-acre property turned out to be a loser. It was too far from the paths of growth, and therefore of zero use to a developer. It couldn't be sold at a profit. The investment team held onto the property, hoping it would rise in value. But, again unfortunately, the team was very inefficient, lacking capable management. Jeanette was committed to paying her one-fourth of the property taxes, but encountered difficulty getting hold of her partners, so property taxes ended up delinquent.[34]

The county government eventually foreclosed on the property for $6,000 in delinquent tax bills.

Amanda had gotten her money out of the property. The team of buyers (including Jeanette) to whom she'd sold the property lost their entire investment.

So be very careful whom you choose as your investment partners. Choose the right ownership entity. And — of course — be 100 percent sure that thorough due diligence has been performed before the purchase!

KEY POINTS TO REMEMBER:

☞ Teaming up with partners is another route to leveraging an investment, and often enables the investor to buy property otherwise unaffordable.

☞ Downsides to investment partnerships are the lack of control the individual investor has, the strong potential for conflicts among partners, and the potential for one or more of the partners to not contribute cash (such as for property taxes) on schedule.

---

[34] Jeanette learned the hard way that a partnership agreement must be thoroughly detailed in writing — with contingencies put in — such as how a partner delinquent in paying his or her share of property taxes will be handled. For example, the delinquent partner's share could have a lien put on it by the other partners.

- The best model for a partnership is having one member be the managing partner (or general partner) legally charged and empowered with managing the investment — from maintenance to marketing to selling — and keeping the others informed.

- The individual investor should only join with partners when a venture is otherwise infeasible due to money or time constraints.

- The author's preference is to join a partnership only under one of the following two arrangements:

  1) One in which he is in 100 percent control as a managing partner with the power of making all decisions.

  2) One in which he has 0 percent control — so he can just park his invested money and allow the other partner or partners to make all the decisions.

- Three common partnership entities are limited partnerships, general partnerships and tenancies in common. Legal advice will help determine the appropriate entity.

- Have a prospectus prepared before pitching an investment to potential partners.

- People to avoid recruiting as partners: over-researchers (who are subject to "analysis paralysis"); the overly emotional; and those who can't afford to risk the amount of money the investment requires.

- People likely to be favorable partners: those prudent in researching an investment, but able to fully commit when ready; those emotionally stable and businesslike; those able to afford a loss but dedicated to seeing the investment reach profitable maturity.

- Investors are difficult to find, and good ones are extremely valuable. They can also become partners in further ventures.

PART THREE

....

THE PROFIT OF LANDBANKING

*When your landbanked parcel rises in stock, you can be sure
the offers will fill your mailbox.*

CHAPTER NINE

Stages of Land Maturity

From the point at which you buy your property, its investment value will progress through several stages before it reaches *maturity* — the point at which you can maximize its profit by selling.

Of course, as with any investment, guesswork is involved. But it will be *educated* guesswork. You can well determine if a sales offer is fair by seeing what comparable properties in the market are selling for. There is always the possibility that by holding onto a property, its value will rise even further; but there is also the risk that its value could fall.[35] If you stand to earn a healthy profit by selling, then your investment is a winner even if the price would have gone up had you held longer.

Following are the seven general stages of land maturity. You might purchase property that is in any of the following stages (except Stage 6, unless you're also a developer); but it is likely you will invest in land in one of the first three stages:

1. **Raw land.** No improvements, such as engineering or grading that has leveled it, are on this pre-development land. Perhaps no utilities, or even paved roads, have reached its vicinity. Maybe it has some form of zoning, such as for agricultural use, or designating the area as desert (which could place restrictions on development to preserve the desert character).

---

[35] Perhaps the area becomes overbuilt and properties suffer high vacancy rates. Perhaps an area's economy grows depressed and demand for housing or commercial space plummets. Perhaps an anti-growth government down-zones property to prevent development. Perhaps the city approves of a homeless shelter or halfway house for paroled criminals to be built in the vicinity. Or perhaps a natural disaster, such as a wildfire or flood, strikes. These are examples of risks, as unlikely as they may be, that could lower a property's value.

2. **In the sphere of influence.** The local city, in its general plan, has identified the land as within its sphere of influence. That means the city intends to extend its borders and services into the area, annexing it within its boundaries and encouraging development.

3. **Zoned for development.** The city or county has rezoned the area of the land to allow development. The zoning could be for any form of residential, commercial or industrial use, or for multi-use. If the property is zoned for residential, the hold is usually shorter than for commercial. The reason: Houses usually come before stores. This doesn't necessarily mean residential zoning is better than commercial. Say housing developments go in around your property that's zoned for commercial. All of a sudden you have a monopoly on coveted commercial space, with developers eager to buy from you because retailers are eager to move in.

4. **Roaded, wired and piped.** Perhaps public streets have now been engineered to the property, power lines have been laid and a water company has extended its pipes into the area. (This stage could come before, after or simultaneously with Stage 5. The property will experience a significant appreciation in value in stages 4 and 5 from the previous stages — which is why the landbanking investor will want to buy *before* these stages.)

5. **Entitled.** "Entitlements" refers to permission from the local government on issues that will further encourage development of the property, and thus increase its value. One form of entitlement is zoning. A property owner could apply to the local government to rezone the property to allow, say, multifamily housing along with single-family residences. (Typically, rezoning is only given in response to plans submitted for a particular development.) Another form of entitlement is having a specific project approved (such as, say, an apartment complex, warehouse or storage facilities). Yet another entitlement is the ability to subdivide the parcel into smaller lots.[36] The process could be relatively short — such as three months — or take years. It depends on the political climate

---

[36] The property owner would likely hire a civil engineer to prepare the plans, tentative map and application.

in the area, especially whether there are environmental concerns expressed by governmental entities and/or grassroots activists, strong anti-growth opposition and a lengthy public-comment process, with hearings and studies required.

There are actually two phases to the entitlement process. The first phase involves securing *tentative approval* from the local government. Tentative approval entails conditions outlined by the government that must be satisfied by the owner for the project to go ahead. (Examples of conditions: putting in a stop sign at an intersection; putting up streetlights; landscaping a portion of the property.) The second phase involves *final approval*. The owner has a civil engineer prepare the plans for the street, utilities and other construction.

The process of securing entitlements involves time and money. The property owner must be prepared to wade through the bureaucracy, including attending city council or county commission meetings when the item is on the agenda. To repeat again the point made about Stage 4: Because a significant increase in value is realized after entitlements are added, a landbanker will want to buy land *before* this stage and add entitlements himself/herself. It is the single best way to boost profit in the investment. If a landbanking investor tries to buy a property that already has entitlements, competition for the purchase will likely come from developers, and the price will shoot up.[37]

If you're concerned that, as a landbanking investor, you'd rather not endure the lengthy process of securing entitlements, you can take heart that you may never have to pursue this avenue. You can just sit on your land and allow rezoning and development to happen all around you, as growth extends into the area, and all property in the area (including yours) goes up in value.

6. **Development.** A developer comes in, buys the land and starts building on it. The landbanker's investment has reached maturity.

---

[37] There is one major exception to the rule about not investing in land after utilities and entitlements have been secured. If a residential development has empty lots for sale, a landbanker could weigh whether these lots are due to greatly increase in value as homes are built. The landbanker should consider trends within the area's real estate market. A lot in, say, an upscale planned community could soar in value as that community is populated and demand for houses there heats up.

7. **Redevelopment.** This is many years down the line, when the structures on a property have aged and fallen in value, and perhaps its location is no longer that attractive because residents or businesses have moved elsewhere. Perfect examples are blighted areas of a city's core. In this stage, a city government will move to buy up or condemn property, bring in developers and have new structures built, such as upscale retail outlets, condominiums or office buildings. (Landbankers may foresee opportunities in such areas and invest in core properties that have declined in value, anticipating renovation efforts.)

The letters start a-comin'

AS THE REAL ESTATE market in which I own a piece of property begins to heat up, with plenty of building activity heading toward my vacant acreage, I'll begin receiving unsolicited offers from agents interested in listing my property. (A listing will be of no expense to you. The agent typically agrees to a listing period, such as 90 days, six months or a year, during which time the agent will represent you in the sale of your property.) They may even try a subtle tack, such as offering to perform a free appraisal of my property. Their hope is that I'll agree to have it listed for sale with them.

I'll also start getting letters or postcards out of the blue from investors. One

---

When unsolicited offers for your property come in the mail, the property is likely a year or two away from shooting up in value. Engage an agent to list the property.

---

postcard was rather cute. It was sent by a married couple whose company's name was four initials. The postcard explained that the initials stood for the first letters in the names of the couple's four children — and then named the children: "Sarah, Rachel, Kody and Ben." (I made up the names, but you get the idea.) I guess you can't blame their parents for trying any angle — even a sappy one!

Here's an excerpt from a form letter that arrived in my mail not long ago:

Dear Land Owner:

Recently while looking through county records, I noticed you own a piece of property in an area in which I am buying property.

Raw land is an interesting thing. If you use it and get to enjoy it, it's great! On the other hand if you don't, it can sometimes feel like an alligator when you get those tax bills every year (or is it twice a year?) — along with the other county fees and/or property owners associations' charges, and let's not forget insurance costs in case someone gets injured on your property when you are not there.

There are definitely pros and cons, and if you are using and enjoying your property, then you should probably throw this letter away. On the other hand, if you're tired of throwing your money out the window then we should probably talk.

I buy land fast and for Cash. I don't play games! We agree on a fair price, a Cash Price. We sign a real simple agreement; I handle all the paperwork and usually in thirty days or less the deal is done. I am not an agent so there are no commissions.

The whole process is very simple, I am a sincere buyer and I think you'll be pleasantly surprised how much I'm willing to pay. I've enclosed a fill-in-the-blanks copy of my purchase agreement with this letter. If you'll please call me on my toll free number above, we can discuss a price that might be acceptable to you. Once we agree on a price, we can just fill in the blanks.

The writer of the above form letter sends these solicitations to owners of vacant land, fully aware that they are not "using" and "enjoying" the property. His letter tries to beat down the value of their land in the owners' minds.

Once in awhile I'll even receive a full, signed offer to purchase. Of course, the offer won't be for what the land is actually worth on the present market. But you can't blame the solicitors for trying. After all, some owners will fall into the trap of selling to a fellow investor, not realizing that the fellow investor could be two years or so ahead of the market zooming upward and trying to get in position to capitalize from it.

What I will do at this point is start monitoring land prices in the area. And I'll engage an agent to list and advertise the property. Experience has taught me that when unsolicited offers begin arriving in my mailbox, the market for the property is likely one or two years away from shooting up.

That's the subject for Chapter Ten.

REPACKAGE AND FLIP

While investors should seek the best properties for landbanking — that is, buildable properties in the path of growth — sometimes land that doesn't have a whole lot of value can become a profitable investment through smart management.

This is akin to the real estate strategy known as "fix and flip," wherein an investor buys a rundown house or building, spruces it up and quickly puts it back on the market at a higher price.

Imagine you buy a piece of raw property for $7,000 in the middle of nowhere, repackage it and promote it better than had the previous owner, and sell it for $15,000. This isn't a far-fetched example.

These opportunities to better market property exist, if you know what to look for and what you're doing. A friend of mine found a lot in Reno, Nevada, that was advertised in one of the free real estate magazines distributed on stands just inside the doors at supermarkets. An older woman had owned the lot for many years. My friend bought it and paid a civil engineer to produce a parcel map to cut the lot into four pieces. The subdivision was approved by the county commission. My friend beefed up the information in an advertisement for the property, and quickly received purchase offers for twice what he paid.

Often, a piece of vacant land is owned by someone who inherited it, and doesn't really know what the land is or could be worth. The owner hires an agent to list the property. (And since the vast majority of real estate agents sell houses, they are unfamiliar with selling land, and therefore not greatly adept at marketing it.) The agent, who already has a full plate, puts minimal information into the advertisement. A savvy landbanker performs due diligence and sees the land as a good opportunity for reaping a short-term profit merely by including more information (gotten from performing legwork) in the advertising. This information could include:

- Water can be drilled and there is a bid for $20,000.
- Power is only 300 feet away and can be brought in for $6,000.
- A septic tank can be put in for $10,000.

Such information — alone — can increase the property's salability, since investors will be more drawn to an ad with such thorough information than an ad with scanty information. Investors scouring ads will see the property as less of a risk, since information is known about it. (Of course, they'll verify the information themselves before making a sales offer.) Were the investors to mentally calculate the value of a property without having information at their fingertips, they would probably overestimate the various costs of bringing in utilities and infrastructure, and the property would be devalued in their minds.

HOW TO CHOOSE A GOOD REAL ESTATE AGENT

You want to hire an agent who is experienced in selling land in the market and has a track record of selling land to investors or developers in that market. So meet with the agent and ask questions. Ask what sales the agent has made. Get a feel for how successful and knowledgeable, active and hardworking the agent is.

Verify the agent's license on the state's Department of Real Estate's website. Check with a local title company or escrow company that the agent is active in the area, and reputable. Just make a few phone calls.

One way to screen agents and choose the best one is to ask several agents to provide broker's price opinions. Call the sales representative of a local title company and ask for several agent references. Perhaps you'll have two or three agents come out to your property. The proper thing to do is to be serious about hiring the best one of these agents. Agents earn their income off of commissions, and their time is valuable. It's not fair to have an agent provide an opinion on a property if you have no intention of hiring the agent, but just want the information for comparison's sake.

There are two major risks for you in hiring a sub-par agent. One is burning up time not selling the property before your agreement with the agent runs out. The other is selling the property for less than what a better agent could have gotten.

A good agent, on the other hand, will truly earn his or her commission, and it will be a win-win situation for both of you.

From personal experience, I recommend you get in writing from an agent what he or she will do for you to market the property. Here are the questions you will ask the agent:

"What will be the contents of the information package you will create?" "How will you deliver it to prospects?" "What signage will you put on the property?" "How will you list the property on the Internet?"

Only after these questions are answered to your satisfaction, in writing, should you sign a listing agreement. In addition, I'll only sign a six-month agreement. Six months should be enough time for an agent to adequately market and sell a property. If the period ends, I can always renew the agreement for an additional period of time — say, another six months.

Homebuilder Hones in on Growing Areas — and the Growth Keeps Coming

When homebuilder Jim Tatum hunts for raw land, he looks for two primary factors: 1) proximity to retail centers, since that indicates where a community's growth is heading; 2) a tentative map for the parcel already approved by the local government, so that Tatum can build more quickly and get his product on the market faster than if he'd have to go through an environmental inspection.

Tatum's strategy works. Developers and operators of retail centers — and the financial institutions that lend to them — thoroughly study an area and its growth potential before committing resources to these costly projects. Therefore, Tatum — doing what any savvy real estate investor should do — piggybacks on the research of these other experts. He lets them perform the due diligence. What's more, he avoids the hassle and long wait — caused by lengthy governmental processes for permission to legally develop a parcel — by buying the parcel *after* it has received its tentative map.

Of course, the landbanker who secures the tentative map will reap the rewards from the subsequent appreciation in value of the property. But Tatum's game isn't landbanking — it's building and selling homes. He enters the picture when it's most advantageous for him to buy a piece of undeveloped but semi-entitled land at its most affordable price, and then sells it as the market of homebuyers begins to reach the area.

Tatum is a second-generation builder who grew up swinging a hammer, working in his father's homebuilding business. Today, he's president of his family-owned American Housing Group, Inc., based in Victorville, California, north of Los Angeles. The company mostly concentrates on building single-family homes. It buys raw land with tentative maps ready to go, gets the other entitlements in place and engineers the lots. It takes about eight months from the point of purchase to having lots ready for building. A recent project of building and selling 22 houses took 18 months from land purchase to sales.

The company primarily focuses on the Southern California market, but has built homes as far north as Bishop, California, and Reno, Nevada. The company's specialty is single-family homes, and its process of searching for optimal sites mirrors that of straightforward landbanking.

"You've got to go to the outskirts where land is available," Tatum says, "and just have to have the foresight, and commonsense, to do all your homework."

TATUM, 67 AND A native of Victorville, continues to be amazed at Southern California's growth, even though throughout his life he's witnessed the phenomenon of areas considered too remote to ever attract residents suddenly escalating in land value as areas closer to cities and towns run out of buildable acreage while the population continues to surge.

Metropolitan Los Angeles (comprised of 49 square miles) ran out of buildable raw land. So did Orange County to the south. "Right now the farmland in Bakersfield is a hot market," Tatum says of the area around the large city that sits toward the southern end of the Golden State's vast Central Valley, on the north side of the mountains separating that valley from the sprawling, heavily populated County of Los Angeles. "If you live in San Fernando Valley (which mostly falls within Los Angeles' city limits, but is many miles north of the urban core), it would take one hour, 15 minutes to get to Bakersfield. Probably 40 percent of home sales are to people who commute back to San Fernando Valley."

Landbankers who bought raw land between the Mojave Desert cities of Victorville and Palmdale — which are, respectively, 80- and 60-mile drives northeast of Los Angeles — and held for 15 to 20 years were enjoying enormous profits in 2005, Tatum notes with surprise. "I went out to look at some land between Victorville and Palmdale, and I was several hours from the nearest houses, and they were asking between $80,000 and $100,000 an acre. It's just desert, not a thing on it. When they bought their land, they paid no more than $2,000 or $3,000 an acre, maximum."

When land prices were depressed in Southern California in the 1990s, "Most builders didn't have the guts or money to buy land," Tatum rues. Still, the resurgence of the real estate market means many landbankers are eager to sell and reap profits. "Now that the market's heated up again, there are a lot of opportunities out there to buy land with tentative maps," he says.

Tatum has found this area between Victorville and Palmdale to have the most affordable buildable acreage in Southern California, and he focuses on buying one-third-acre lots with tentative maps approved. His business plan in 2005 was buying lots for $35,000 apiece and building houses with three bedrooms, two baths and two-car garages, with from 1,650 to 2,000 square feet of floor space. The homes are designed in the Southwestern architectural style with tile roofs, stucco exteriors and fenced, landscaped front yards with Kentucky bluegrass. They sold for up to $315,000. And there was a constant stream of buyers — a mix of first-time homebuyers, and locals who'd sold their older houses in town for profits and were converting the equity into homes in newer neighborhoods farther out.

The profit margins remain favorable for small builders such as himself, Tatum says. "You can't put your money anywhere else and get that kind of leverage." But prudent selection of land sites still is critical — just as it is for traditional landbanking investors.

The path of growth is fairly simply to predict in the Victorville area, given the natural barrier of the Mojave River, which forces any growth to the west or north, Tatum points out. And, again, he takes advantage of research already completed by financial-lending institutions, developers and investors, by choosing homebuilding sites near retail centers.

But any investor should adequately answer for himself or herself the basic questions before sinking money into a site:

How far away is development at present?

What is the location and state of the water system, sewer system and roads?

Is the site in the direction of the nearest town's growth?

Optimism, alone, about the booming Southern California market can't turn a land purchase into a sound investment.

"I've seen guys go way out there in the desert," Tatum says, "and think the growth is going to reach it someday."

Again — while raw land is available on the outskirts of burgeoning communities in once-remote areas, in the path of these communities' growth — raw land ALSO is available at greater distances where the growth may never reach.

To reiterate Tatum's advice: You as the investor have "to have the foresight, and commonsense, to do all your homework."

KEY POINTS TO REMEMBER:

☛ There are seven general stages of land maturity. Landbankers typically invest in land in one of the first three of the following stages:

1) Raw land.
2) Land identified in the city's sphere of influence.
3) Zoned for development.
4) Roads engineered and power, water and sewer lines reach the area.
5) Entitlements, such as zoning favorable to development, or permission to subdivide the property, have been secured.
6) Development.
7) Redevelopment.

☛ The arrival of unsolicited offers from agents to list the property, and offers from investors to buy the property, signal that the market is likely a year or two from shooting upward.

☞ An exception to the rule that profit comes from waiting for a property to mature is a method of buying poorly marketed raw land, repackaging it and selling it for a quick profit. This is a "repackage and flip" strategy, similar to "fix and flip" with houses.

☞ The optimal agent to sell a property is an agent with a good track record of selling land in the specific market to developers or investors.

The more useful information put into your ad, the better your property will stand out on the market.

CHAPTER TEN

The Sale Is the Key

The critical time for realizing a profit on a landbanked investment is when you *sell*. This is even more important than when you buy. As long as you pay a reasonable price for a property that meets the criteria of a sound investment, you are fairly well assured that the property will appreciate in value.

Selling, then, is the key. You don't want to sell too soon, and you don't want to sell too late. And you sure as heck don't want to sell without realizing a profit.

Many small land investors don't focus on the inevitable sale when they buy a piece of property. They look to pick up a parcel at a good market price, without thinking far enough ahead to the end result. I was that way, of course, as a naïve 21-year-old excited about buying my 2½ acres out in the Mojave Desert. I was elated to be getting into the game. Now I was a landowner! Investing in land was the smart thing to do! But I didn't have a solid exit strategy. In fact, I had *no* exit strategy.

When buying land, think about who will buy it from you down the road. The sale is the key to profit.

As I described in this book's introduction, all I looked ahead to was some vague distant future when my lot would be developed on a gleaming new cul-de-sac of whitewashed adobe houses with pink-tiled roofs, peopled by happy suburban families. And that, sadly, never happened. Residential developers never moved to build among the sagebrush and Joshua trees a half-hour out of the small desert town of Adelanto. San Bernardino County eventually turned the area into a park with dirt-bike trails and paid me 56 percent of the price I'd bought the lot for.

Investors of all ages succumb to this shortsightedness. They're so wrapped up in the act of buying land that they don't formulate a plan for converting it into a profit. Consider the 58-year-old insurance agent from the San Francisco Bay area, mentioned in Chapter Four, who anted up $83,500 from his retirement savings for 10 acres south of Reno, Nevada — an area booming in population and commerce. He was so confident about the value of buying in that soaring real estate market that he didn't even bother visiting the site of his parcel until the sale was nearly complete. When he did check his nest egg out, he found it to be strewn with big rocks, and on a slope far steeper than he'd imagined from looking at the photograph his real estate agent had shown him. Even then, he said he still had "a good feeling" about his investment's rich potential.

When you buy land, you have to think about whom you're going to sell it to down the road. *A homebuilder? A big development firm? Another small investor?* You've got to ask yourself: Who is going to want this property and provide me with a profit? And what evidence do I have — based on my due diligence — that this property possesses intrinsic value for a particular buyer, and that such a buyer is going to come along within the next three, five, seven, 10, 12, 15 or 20 years? (You adjust your thinking to your personal investment timetable.)

Like any entrepreneur preparing a business plan, you've got to zero in on the market for your business. Who are the customers going to be? As a landbanker, your business is the piece of land you're investing in.

Now, there are landbankers who are content with buying and holding, just to see how the market develops. They're capable of carrying the expenses of the property, including paying taxes on it. Maybe they're sheer speculators with disposable income to wager with. Or maybe they're interested in bequeathing the property to their heirs, passing it down as a legacy in their estate. That's fine for them.

But when it comes to hard-nosed, businesslike landbanking — the subject of this book — investing in land is no exercise in wishful thinking. Your due diligence will reveal not only the current value of the property in question, but how its value will increase from being in the path of growth, when that growth is likely to arrive, what entitlements the property could or should accrue — and what type of buyer will end up tendering an offer.

WHO will want this property, and WHY will they want it?

After you've found a piece of ground, researched it and swung the financing to buy it, your concentration will center on selling it when the time is right. You'll be keeping an eye on the growth pattern of the area. If the years go by and there's no movement in the market and your property's value doesn't appreciate, maybe you'll decide you don't care to wait for the land to fully mature, and you want to divest of it and move those funds into a quicker investment. But if and when the market does begin to percolate, you'll be watching your property's value more closely — eyes fixed on the sweet prize: the sale.

You'll calculate what sales price will yield you a desired return on your cumulative investment (the purchase price plus taxes, fees and other expenses you've paid out over the period you've held the property, plus commissions, fees and capital gains paid from the sale). And you'll gauge just how great a return you should reasonably expect.

Again: The sale is the key.

It's time to list when the market heats up

WHEN I SEE REAL estate prices steadily rising in a market in which I'm landbanking a piece of property, I'll prepare to list the property with a broker or agent specializing in land.[38] I'll know that the market is moving toward a peak.

I'll find the best possible agent. Of course, as mentioned in Chapter Nine, I want someone who knows the local market, is experienced in the local market, and specializes in land. The same real estate license can allow an agent to sell a home or a piece of land. But selling residential property and selling vacant land

---

[38] A real estate "agent" is tested and licensed by the state, while a "broker" has taken an additional test and is authorized to run a private real estate firm. Incidentally, a Realtor (the word is capitalized) is a licensed real estate professional who is a member of the National Association of Realtors.

are two different specialties. In hot real estate markets, the competition for clients among agents can grow very fierce. All agents are looking for listings. Some may tell you they specialize in land, but it's up to you to determine that they really do. Some may even tell you they already have a buyer for your property (and perhaps they do).

Remember: We're living in an age of specialization — whether the field is law, medicine or automotive repair. (For example, you would see a probate attorney for matters related to estates, and a personal-injury attorney after an automobile accident.) Ask agents what property they've sold recently. Go on-line and see what listings they have for vacant land. Ask which builders and developers they market to. If an agent doesn't market to builders and developers, the agent may not be right to represent your property.

> *We're living in an age of specialization. If an agent doesn't market to builders and developers, the agent may not be right to represent your property.*

Make no doubt about it, you will need an agent to sell your property. A good agent is fully worth the commission. A good agent knows the market, the property values, the players. Land is seldom sold by sticking a for-sale sign in front of it. An agent doesn't get paid until a sale is complete. Therefore, an agent will aggressively court solid potential buyers, and navigate the sale through to its completion.

Agents have a lot more work to do in selling land than in selling a home and posting for-sale signs. To interest buyers, agents have to assemble detailed binders packaged with information about the property. And an agent may produce dozens or even hundreds of these binders to send to potential buyers — the active builders and developers in an area. Therefore, commissions paid to agents by sellers on land sales are typically about 10 percent — but like all commission rates, they are negotiable between the agent and client.

Now, an agent can't be expected to do all the work. Yours is surely just one of the properties the agent is representing. If you want to gain the most from your investment, you should partner closely with your agent. You'll need to make yourself easily accessible, keeping lines of communication open regarding purchase offers and any complications that could arise. You'll also need to provide the agent with as complete information as possible about the property for the agent's marketing package.

In Chapter Nine I noted that the more useful details a seller includes in advertising a property, the more interest the property will spark in serious investors. After all, investors pore through countless ads in buyer's guides and real estate listings. They're thinking ahead to what they can make on a property, and how much money and work they'll have to sink into it in the meantime. This is especially true

The more pertinent information provided about your property, the more it will attract a buyer and stand out from poorly advertised properties.

of developers. They conservatively calculate the costs of bringing in utilities and infrastructure. They can't afford to underestimate, so they must overestimate.

The more pertinent information you can communicate about your property, the more it will attract a developer or other buyer looking for such a property. And the more your property will stand out from properties advertised with scanty information. This pertinent information can include:

- A general description of the area, including the population and economic growth of the local municipality; the municipality's history; its chief industries and cultural and recreational amenities; and the property's location within the municipality's sphere of influence.
- Current zoning.
- Applications for rezoning (which may be pending with the local city or county).
- Exact distance to current or officially planned power, water and sewer lines.
- Bids received from contractors to improve the property, such as for sinking a well or extending power to the property.
- Nearby building projects approved by the city or county.

- Announced plans of coming development. (For example, has a housing developer or a major retailer issued media releases, or applied for permits, to build nearby? Or has the local school district board been discussing — or has it even approved — construction of a new school in the area?)
- Approvals, including tentative approvals, by the city or county for building on the property.
- Conditions the city or county has set in a tentative approval for building on the property. (Conditions could include a requirement to put in curbs or gutters, a stop sign, crosswalk or traffic light, a noise-abatement wall or landscaping, and so on.)
- Fees charged by the city or county during the application and building processes, including application, plan-check, development and park fees.
- The preliminary title report from a title company, proving the seller is the rightful owner and listing any debtor claims against the property. Normally, a preliminary title report is issued right before the transaction moves to closing. Obtaining the report ahead of time can be very valuable to the seller, because it can further hook a serious buyer's interest.

In sum: The more thorough your disclosure about your property, the less risk perceived by potential buyers, and the more valuable your property becomes.[39]

The four stages of a sale

FOLLOWING ARE THE FOUR general stages of a landbank sale:

1. **Holding while the property appreciates.** The property is not yet ready to sell for a profit, even if offers come in. Unless the investor must liquidate the property due to financial constraints, the investor continues to hold.

2. **Market percolates.** The property is appreciating. Growth is quickly approaching or has reached the area. There may be rezoning to facilitate development. Feelers and

---

[39] The land owner would do will to examine several different marketing packages for different properties, to ascertain the information necessary for a good package.

low-ball offers are coming in, often by form letters, from opportunists. Some offers may be verbal — to measure your response. Other offers may be in the form of a "letter of intent," a non-obligating document preceding an official offer, specifying what the buyer is willing to do (such as putting money into an escrow account for a period of time to complete due diligence, with the money refundable by a certain date), and what the buyer is looking for (such as confirmation of title and other facts about the property). Agents are asking to list the property. Some may even claim to have buyers for it. This may be the time to hire an agent. Often (as mentioned in Chapter Nine), the market is one or two years away from seeing prices sharply rise.

3. **Seller's market.** Property values have risen, as evidenced by the listed and sales prices of comparable properties ("comps"). If an agent hasn't already been hired, now is the time. The agent prepares and disseminates a detailed listing and a detailed package. The listed price leaves room for negotiation with a buyer. Serious offers, in the form of a letter of intent or an actual offer to purchase, come in — each one good for a period of time. The owner considers whether the market is up and coming, and if so, resists jumping at the first solidly financed offer (unless that offer is so attractive that it yields or exceeds the degree of profit the owner is seeking).[40]

4. **The sale.** An offer is accepted. The deal goes into escrow. The sale is consummated. Agents' fees are paid. The investor realizes a profit and decides whether to pay capital-gains tax or defer the taxes by rolling over the profit in a 1031 exchange.[41]

---

[40] Land sales are usually slower than home sales. A homeowner may entertain two or three offers in a single day, if the market is hot. Typically, land for sale receives far fewer offers, and are much more spaced out in time. Also, the process of completing a land transaction is more complicated than a house sale, and therefore takes more time.

[41] A 1031 exchange, so named because it is allowed under Section 1031 of the Internal Revenue Code, is a tax-deferral strategy that permits reinvesting profits from a property sale into a "like-kind" property. Also known as a "Starker exchange" because of the case that precipitated the law, a 1031 rollover must be into property in the United States of equal or greater value than the property sold. The replacement property must be identified by the buyer within 45 days and received within 180 days. Any leftover money ("the boot") from the property sale not used in the rollover can be taxed. The foregoing is general information; a qualified accountant should be consulted before pursuing a 1031 exchange. There also are businesses that handle the legal paperwork for 1031s. One business, Investment Property Exchange Services, Inc., has this website: www.ipx1031.com.

My personal philosophy, after nearly two decades in landbanking, is that the seller and the buyer should each gain from the sale. That means, "Take a little, leave a little." Don't try to chisel every last red cent out of a sale. If I've had a property for sale for a reasonable amount of time and a generous offer has come in, I don't try to hold out in hopes that an even more handsome offer will appear. (After all, even if such an offer were to come, who's to say I wouldn't refuse *it* and keep holding out for yet a better one?) I realize that each party wants to maximize his/her profit. And, after all, I'm eager to take my profit and reinvest it in another pre-developed property that stands to earn me income upon maturity. That's my position in the ballgame.

In addition to the purchase price, the biggest consideration in reviewing an offer is the strength of the buyer's *financing*. In the best-case scenario, payment will be in cash. That means there's zero risk to you, the seller. The cleaner the deal, the better. In the worst-case scenario, the offer is heavily financed, the source or sources of financing aren't stable (say, a private individual is footing much of the bill), and payment will be made over a prolonged length of time.

The seller must avoid letting a buyer of questionable means tie up the property in escrow, taking the property off the market for that period, with slim chance of closing escrow with a sale. This sort of buyer may be trying to flip the property — setting up his/her own buyer to turn a quick profit. If that strategy falls through, you may be able to recoup money forfeited by the buyer in escrow. (The jargon in the real estate business is "money going hard" — meaning that money the buyer put in escrow will not be refunded by the seller after the specified time limit is exhausted.)[42] But you've also lost precious time in having the property on the market for serious buyers. What can happen in this scenario is that the 60 or 90 days of escrow time elapses, and the buyer requests an additional 60 or 90 days. Before you know it, four to six months have gone by. And the buyer may request yet *another* extension . . .

---

[42] My custom is to insist that a portion of a buyer's escrow money during the due-diligence period "goes hard" after 45 days. If the buyer requests a time extension for due diligence, I'll ask that an additional amount of money be paid me to grant that extension. My aim is not to penalize and take advantage of the buyer, but to ensure my property isn't needlessly tied up when it could be on the market attracting buyers. In effect, I'm allowing the buyer to buy an option on buying my property.

That's why, when I'm selling a property, I put on my detective's hat. I'll carefully review the buyer's financial position. I'll ask for personal references. (A developer, for example, may list bank officers, title-company officials, real estate brokers or contractors as business references.) I'll ask the buyer what his/her intention is with the property. I'll want to know whom I'm selling to. I want to avoid being strung along. I want to ensure the buyer is capable of closing.

Not too long before I wrote these words, I had a piece of property up for sale. The buyer's offer seemed like a good number to me. But the offer was contingent upon the buyer receiving a bank loan. Therefore, I asked which bank was involved, and what was the loan-to-value. I wanted to make sure the figures added up. They

---

Carefully review the buyer's financial position. Ask for references. Ask what the buyer's intention is with the property. And ensure the buyer is capable of closing.

---

did. But if they hadn't, I would have rejected the offer. After all, I wasn't desperate to sell. Patience is a virtue in investing.

This brings me to another vital point: Offers are good for a period of time, but you do have some wiggle room. You can inform a prospective buyer that you need more time to consider the offer. You don't want speed working against you. As a rule, if a buyer is trying to rush negotiations, slow it down a little bit. After all, the buyer isn't the only one who will need to perform due diligence. You, the seller, need to investigate the buyer. And you'll also need to take a second look at the market. Remember, prices fluctuate. You need to determine whether your property is really listed at the market value, or not.

Professionalism separates landbankers from landowners

THE FOUR STAGES OF a sale outlined above are those that a true landbank investor goes through with a property. There are "landbankers," and then there are "landbankers by accident." The latter just sell a property as is, with no improvements made to it, and little attempt given to boosting its value through homework and thoroughly detailed advertising. The landbankers by accident likely came into the property through inheritance or some other indirect fashion, or perhaps bought it many years before when land was cheap, and just happened to hold onto it. The course of events led to the property's value appreciating. The owner himself/herself didn't invest any effort into adding value.

But the true landbanker is businesslike about the property from the purchase, through the hold, through the sale. The true landbanker increases the property's value through making improvements or doing the legwork to inform buyers why the property is valuable.

The true landbanker is focused on maximizing the profit from the property. The true landbanker is a *professional*.

SHOULD YOU FINANCE A BUYER'S PURCHASE?

Seller financing was discussed in Chapter Seven. To repeat: When you buy vacant land, you may find that your best option is to have the purchase financed by the seller. Not only can you negotiate a better interest rate than what a bank or other financial institution can offer you, but you can have a greater portion of the purchase (say, 80 to 90 percent) financed by the seller, whereas a bank may only cover 30 to 50 percent of the "loan to value."

But now that *you're* the seller, do you want to finance your buyer's purchase? Consider that this may be the only way for the buyer to swing the deal.

If you decide to carry the buyer's loan, what you'll be after in the contract (which you'll have drawn up by an escrow company) is as large a down payment as possible, and as much security as possible.[43] By "security" I mean the level of monthly payments the buyer commits to make, and what collateral (such as equity in a home) the buyer can attach to the deal. These two considerations — down payment and security — will help you determine whether the purchase offer is acceptable. It also will help you choose which buyer to deal with, if you receive multiple offers.

Let's say I get an offer of $100,000 for a small, undeveloped lot. The buyer offers a 10 percent down payment ($10,000); that leaves $90,000 as the principal of the loan. The annual interest rate is agreed on: 10 percent. We also agree on minimum payments of $1,000 a month. That would mean the buyer — who would have to cover compound interest on the principal — would finish payments in 14 years, if paying $1,000 a month. The offer seems reasonable, but I want to ensure the buyer will stick with the payments and not force me to foreclose on the property at some point. Foreclosing is a hassle.

My first question: "Do you own your own home?"

If the answer is yes, I'll ask, "How much is your home worth?"

Let's say the answer is "$400,000." My next question: "How much do you owe on it?"

Let's say the answer is, "$325,000."

That means the buyer has $75,000 in equity built up.

I'll say: "I'll sell you my land. But look, I want to make sure I get paid. And you want to buy the property. So I want to cross-collateralize your home to make sure you pay."

That means if the buyer quits making payments on the property, I'd foreclose on the property and, if the balance of payments was large enough, take ownership of the buyer's home, too.

That's a strong incentive for the buyer to keep current with payments!

This may seem like a hardball business decision, but the buyer is asking me, the seller, to carry his loan. That puts me in the position of being a bank.

Incidentally, earlier in my landbanking career I was in a weak financial position

---

[43] The cost of having an escrow company draw up a sales contract is based upon the price of the property. Expect to pay from $300 to $1,000.

in which, as a buyer, I could only come up with a relatively small down payment such as 10 percent, and sellers would demand additional security, too. I always made sure that I could well afford monthly payments on investment properties.

One more point: As a seller, you don't want to structure your loans to buyers in such a way that it will not be a long time before the buyer begins to build equity in the property. If the buyer's monthly payments are mostly covering interest, and not chipping away at the principal of the loan, the buyer could end up walking away from the property, leaving you to foreclose on it. I also don't require pre-payment penalties. If the buyer wishes to pay off the loan sooner — so be it!

Sitting with the buyer, I'll write down the details of the deal — the total purchase price, down payment, term of the loan (such as 10 years), minimal monthly payments, no pre-payment penalty, how the buyer intends to take title (such as in his or her name), how my name is on the title, and the assessor's parcel number on the property.

With this information to supply, I give it to my broker or agent and ask that a set of instructions for a sales contract be written.

Finally, I'll have my note serviced by a note-collection business. Say a buyer is going to pay you, the seller, with a $20,000 down payment, followed by payments of $1,000 a month. You don't want these checks coming directly to you. You want the checks going to an independent, third-party collection agency. That protects you by having a record maintained of payments (including reports for the IRS), having a professional party ensure payments are made (sending out monthly statements, calling on late payments and abiding by collection laws). The note-collection service can also handle the process of foreclosure if necessary.

For this service, you'll pay a fee based on the amount of money the note-collecting business is collecting. I've found this to be well worth the price.

A Fruitful Investment in an Orange Grove

Ron Kemper hit pay dirt with his very first land purchase, while still in high school, but didn't even know it. The teenager could not — in his wildest dreams — have conceived of how enormous the value would end up appreciating on the 10-acre orange grove he bought in the San Bernardino, California, suburb of Highland from the woman who'd hired him to irrigate the soil and burn smudge pots to prevent the fruit buds from freezing.

Back in 1973, the land, according to area Realtors, was worth $6,000 an acre. Kemper didn't have $6,000 in savings — much less the $60,000 the entire 10 acres would cost at market value. The landowner recognized this, and also that the young man who had worked her orchard for two years was industrious and ambitious. So she offered to sell him the 10 acres at $8,000 an acre — $2,000 per acre above market value — but with a payment plan that would enable him to buy. She asked for no money down, offered a low 6 percent interest rate and agreed that Kemper could make his annual payment after selling the year's crop of navel oranges.

Kemper agreed. He knew he could generate a cash flow from the orchard. He was the kind of hustling kid who stands out from the pack in every neighborhood — the kid who always finds a way to earn money on his own, instead of relying on an allowance. At age 11, young Ron was leading trail rides at area dude stables. At 13, he was the exercise boy giving horses workouts at the local racetrack. He also shod horses at the track and surrounding ranches. By 16, he'd bought a new Chevrolet pickup — paying cash.

Kemper's parents were real estate brokers, but he didn't seek their advice before buying the orange grove. After making the purchase he did offer them, as well as his siblings, the opportunity to join in the investment, but none bought in. Still, they were supportive.

Ron got to work tending to his oranges. He worked the grove himself — irrigating, spraying for pests, pruning the trees, smudging. At harvest time he solicited bids from packing houses owned by big companies such as Dole and Sunkist, plus a couple independents. They'd send picking crews. With the profits, Kemper covered his mortgage payments. He also worked construction jobs, and took night classes in junior college to better educate himself. At 20, he earned his real estate license and went to work at his parents' brokerage; the income helped him pay off his 10-acre investment.

In all, it took 15 years for Kemper to own the property free and clear. He had long planned to build his principal residence there, and that's exactly what he did in 1988. As he recalls, "It was where I thought I wanted to live and spend the rest of my life. It wasn't a true investment. I simply wanted it."

For the next 15 years, the house in Highland was where Ron, his wife and three children called home. In the meantime, he forged ahead in his real estate career, as broker-owner of Kemper Real Estate, investing in land in California and Nevada, Arizona and Idaho.

Southern California land values also forged ahead — including his 10 acres bought at age 18. "It was a decent property that I held for 30 years without ever considering selling it until the area got developed to where it wouldn't fit the lifestyle I wanted," Kemper says.

He bought 300 acres in Big Bear, California, and built his current home so he could once again enjoy a rural environment. When he sold the 10 acres in Highland in 2004 to a land speculator, that original $80,000 investment fetched $3 million.

FOR KEMPER, THE MORAL of the story is: "Some of your best investments you do by accident."

It worked out because he'd bought the orange grove to hold. And that plan — serendipitously — capitalized on the magic of landbanking:

"Any time you can buy in the path of progress and have a 10-, 20- or 30-year hold program, you should reap huge profits."

In his three-plus decades of real estate investing, Kemper has bought pieces of land specifically as investments to sell when the time was right. He's solved the development problems associated with making each of his investment parcels buildable — engineering them, securing entitlements such as zoning, marketing them and, typically, reselling each one after three or five years. That's true landbanking. It requires strategy and patience.

In contrast, anyone buying land to "spin it" in six months is risking a backfiring investment, Kemper says. "If you only plan on carrying a piece of property for six months and aren't successful in your marketing plan or getting it entitled, then you have a huge alligator."

In his long career, Kemper has seen — over and over — shortsighted investors trip themselves up being over-eager and ill-prepared to nurse an investment to maturity.

He still marvels at his beginner's luck with the orange grove. "One of my best investments was simply a passive investment. Something I simply wanted to build a home on."

KEY POINTS TO REMEMBER:

- Before and after buying property, the landbanker should be focused on whom the eventual buyers will be.
- The sale is the key to the profit, even more than the purchase.
- An agent is indispensable in marketing and selling property, but the seller should work as closely as possible with the agent to facilitate the process.

☛ The more pertinent details about a property in an advertisement, the more investors will be attracted. Information can include:

1) A general description of the area.
2) Current zoning.
3) Applications for rezoning.
4) Exact distance to current or planned power, water and sewer lines.
5) Bids from contractors to improve the property.
6) Nearby building projects.
7) Coming developments.
8) Tentative or final approvals for entitlements.
9) Conditions for a tentative approval.
10) Governmental fees for building.
11) The preliminary title report.

☛ The four general stages of a sale:

1) The hold for appreciation.
2) The market heats up.
3) Seller's market.
4) The sale.

☛ Providing financing to a buyer should be based on collecting as large a down payment as possible, and as much security as possible. Your broker or agent can prepare the sales contract.

☛ An investor providing seller financing should have the note serviced by a note-collection business, which will collect payment checks.

Take care of your property while it's landbanked,
and when its value rises it will take care of you.

CHAPTER ELEVEN

Managing the Investment

While a landbanking investor waits for the property to mature in value to its optimal price for sale, the property must be managed. Sometimes this is as simple as maintaining a good mailing address (pay those post-office box fees if you have one) and regularly checking and handling the correspondence that comes to this address for the property's owner listed with the local government. One reason landbanking is attractive is that it is generally low maintenance. There are no tenants to tend to, as in a rental property. There is no cash flow. But there *are* bills to pay:

- Property taxes. Expect to pay twice a year. Becoming delinquent can mean the city or county attaching a lien to the property, and eventually foreclosing and auctioning it off.

- Any finance payments. These are probably paid monthly to the lender. Defaulting can mean the creditor foreclosing.

- Any expenses related to keeping the land free from health or safety hazards and complying with city or county codes. Codes typically range from ensuring no trash or junk accumulates from illegal dumping, to preventing weeds from turning the ground into a mini-jungle. As growth nears the property, the local fire, health or land-use department may send a letter declaring that weeds must be abated.

- Fencing and posting no-trespassing signs. These can be a simple precaution against intruders, and can help limit the owner's liability in the event an interloper gets injured on the property, sets a fire or causes some other nuisance or damage.

- Liability insurance. Vacant land typically doesn't pose too much of a risk to a landowner, but the extra layer of protection from vacant-land insurance is not a bad option for guarding against a worst-case scenario, such as a child trespassing on the land and getting seriously injured. Vacant-land insurance often can be added on to a basic homeowner's policy for a minor charge. Ironically, a landowner's chance of getting sued increases by carrying insurance, since a plaintiff's attorney will then have a deep pocket (the insurance company) to aim for. But the landowner's assets should be protected.

You should visit the property at least once a year, just to keep an eye on it and make sure all is well within the property boundaries. You want to ensure no one is squatting on it and no illegal structures (such as lean-tos) have been erected. (The local government could require you to remove such.) Also, while there normally won't be any cause for concern, there is a legal concept known as "prescriptive easement." For example, a neighbor could, without permission, continually use an

---

Visit the property at least once a year, and make sure all is well within the boundaries.

---

area encroaching on your property as an easement (such as a road or an irrigation ditch) for a period of time specified by state law, and thus legally establish and acquire that easement for himself/herself. Or hikers, cyclists or equestrians could use your property as a shortcut, over and over again, and thus establish the path as a right-of-way falling within the public domain. To prevent this, the landowner can erect a fence, post no-trespassing signs and send a certified letter advising trespassers or squatters to cease and desist.

Finally, the local real estate market must be monitored. Not intensively, however, until growth begins to reach the area and the market begins percolating. But it's not a bad idea to keep a thumb on the pulse by checking out comparable properties ("comps") once or twice a year, to chart prices of these parcels of similar size and location as yours.

If you're the general or managing partner in a partnership or investment group, you'll send out an update letter to fellow investors twice a year (coinciding with property taxes) to keep them apprised of the investment's progress. (You'll also have to collect their share of the tax payments at this time.)

But mostly, you don't need to pay a lot of attention to the land during this early stage of maturity, when you're just holding while the property appreciates.

Managerial duties shift as market value increases

INEVITABLY, UNLESS THE LAND is not a good investment, growth will draw nearer to the property. The market is percolating. An early sign is when notices arrive from the local city or county government announcing projects up for approval in the vicinity of the property, and giving the time, dates and locations of public hearings.[44] Another sign (as described in chapters Nine and Ten) is letters from real estate agents interested in listing the property (or offering to perform a free appraisal), and letters (usually form letters) from investors feeling out your interest in selling.

This correspondence should be kept on file. It's a way of tracking the property's appreciation in value. Similarly, any information on roads and utilities being improved or extended to the area of your property should be filed away.

Now the investor begins paying more attention to the local market — what's being built where, and by whom; what zoning changes are taking place; the prices, and days on the market, of comps. The property is drawing lots of attention on the market.

And then it becomes a seller's market, with rising property values. Form-letter offers are now coming in to buy the property (as described in Chapter Ten). This means investors or even builders are blanketing the area, trying to buy up as much

---

[44] You don't need to attend these hearings, unless you have time on your hands. If you're interested, you can check whether the hearings' minutes are posted afterward on the government's website; you also could call the government's clerk's office and ask that the minutes be mailed to you. The minutes will include whether the project was approved, and public comments about the project.

land as they can. The time is getting ripe for development. The value of your property is rapidly maturing.

If not done already, this is the time to hire an agent to list the property. (As mentioned in Chapter Ten, you'll want an agent who specializes in land, is experienced in your property's market and — optimally — has connections to builders, developers or investors buying land in the area.) Unlike houses, land just isn't typically sold with a for-sale sign and flier box posted in front of it.

If you're managing the property for a group of investors, this is the time to let your partners know that the property is actively being marketed. Communication is key. And if the partnership or group agreement specifies that decisions such as accepting a sales offer must be put to a vote, obviously communication is essential. Because your investment is now in its final stage of maturity.

Managing the sales process was described in Chapter Ten.

And when you sell the property for a good profit — congratulations. You earned it!

It Isn't the Business, but the Building Housing It and the Land Beneath It, That Bring in the Big Bucks

Ken Bogart was gung-ho to succeed in business when he started his fabric store with $3,000 of capital in 1973 in Reno, Nevada. "We worked for free for the first two years, no income, and worked night jobs to support the business," he says of his wife and himself.

Then a friend in Lewiston, Idaho, caught the entrepreneurial bug and asked Bogart and his father-in-law if they'd open a store with him in that town. They hunted for a building to rent. They found a one-story, 9,000-square-foot building downtown that had been a dime store. It turned out to be cheaper to buy the building outright than pay the monthly rent on it. So that's what Bogart and his

---

father-in-law did, becoming 50-50 co-owners.

"We bought the building totally by accident, just unplanned," Bogart recalls. His father-in-law put up the money, and Bogart borrowed his half of the purchase cost from his father-in-law and paid interest. Their friend in Lewiston paid the two partners rent.

Back in Reno, the building they'd been renting suddenly became unavailable. The landlord informed them a week before Christmas that he intended to tear the building down and build a sporting-goods store. He'd previously promised, verbally, to give them three months' notice before any eviction. Instead, he had the roof torn off the building on New Year's Day.

It was a bitter, but invaluable, lesson about the privileges of land ownership. Bogart found a 16,000-square-foot building to rent three miles away. But up in Idaho, he kept on buying. He and his partner from Lewiston went on to co-own fabric stores not only in Lewiston, but Burley, Garden City, Idaho Falls, Jerome and Pocatello. Bogart owned the buildings and the land beneath them. And after he sold the businesses to his partner in 1996, Bogart hung onto the real property.

"It's a monthly income from the rentals," he says. "The buildings pay for themselves, and the building assets appreciate."

MEANWHILE, BOGART WATCHED THE fabric industry change. His store in Reno sells fabric primarily to women who make clothes for their families or clubs, or sew uniforms or Halloween costumes. The store also sells upholstery, decorating materials and accompanying supplies.

Outsourcing of labor by domestic clothing manufacturers, however, has made clothes from retail outlets relatively inexpensive — which has hurt the market for customers who make their own clothes, Bogart says.

"It was a great business in the 1980s, and an OK business in the early '90s," he says. "It's a dying industry now because companies pay 10 cents an hour to people in China to sew clothes."

That reality underscores a larger lesson about running a small business, he says. "You make a living from the business — but the buildings and the land beneath them provide your future, your retirement."

Further illustrating this lesson is Bogart's property-buying experience in the vicinity of the site where his store stands in an industrial zone. A block west, he bought a bare corner lot with the idea of constructing a building on it to house his store if the rent at its current site ever were raised. Then he had a further idea. A 16,000-square-foot warehouse was next to the empty lot, occupying 1 ½ acres. He bought that, too, and renovated it. The bare lot became parking for his store, while the warehouse was rented to automotive shops — providing cash flow while the building and its land continue to appreciate in value.

While many landbankers search for parcels outside towns, in the path of growth, Bogart has developed an eye for distressed property in the middle of town. This is "in-fill" property.

"I'm looking to get into more aggressive development," he says.

There's more money, it seems, in brick and dirt than in cloth.

Monitor the market by checking comps periodically.

KEY POINTS TO REMEMBER:

☞ Managing a property until the sales phase involves:
1) Maintaining a good mailing address.
2) Paying bills — property taxes, finance payments, maintenance expenses and, perhaps, liability insurance.
3) Fencing and signing the property to keep out trespassers and prevent health or safety hazards such as trash dumping.

4) Visiting the property at least once a year to ensure it is safe and also that no one is encroaching on its boundaries (such as with roads or ditches) or using it for shortcuts — possible steps toward eroding your property rights through prescriptive easement.

5) Monitoring the local real estate market.

6) Filing all correspondence, such as notices of public hearings for development in the area, and offers from agents or investors.

7) Hiring a real estate agent to list the property as the market heats up.

Shoulda, coulda, wish I woulda . . . bought that lot when it was empty.

CHAPTER TWELVE

Shoulda, Coulda, Wish I Woulda

I nvestor's remorse is a natural byproduct of the speculation game. Some risks are rewarded, others not. Good land, by its nature, will almost always appreciate in value, and the risk of loss is low. But investor's remorse can come from missed opportunities for further profit — such as by selling too soon, or passing over one property for a different one that ends up not earning as much, or not having the resources or knowledge to have gotten into the game earlier, or in a different region. Or simply (and perhaps most common of all) not having seized an opportunity when it was there in front of you.

You slap your forehead and think, "Shoulda, coulda, wish I woulda."

I mentioned in this book's introduction how my family would drive down Beach Boulevard in Southern California back in the 1970s, and my dad would reminisce about how this old Highway 39 — now a bustling four-to six-lane thoroughfare with mile after mile of development — had nothing but farmland and open space on either side back in the '50s and '60s. Other times, he'd talk about beachfront lots in pricey Orange County going for only $2,500 or so back in the day. He'd rue: "It takes two things at the same time, and I never had 'em at the same time: forethought and money."

Shoulda, coulda, wish I woulda.

In the introduction I also explained how, as a young man, I vowed to not miss out on investing in land and the enormous profits to be reaped by getting into the game early in a promising area before the masses discovered it. And so I slapped my meager savings down on a couple acres of distant, sun-baked desert that a kindly older gentleman in a shiny late-model Lincoln Continental ran an advertisement for in the newspaper.

Lesson learned! In the ensuing years I gained an understanding of the landbanking game. I mastered the steps necessary to ferreting out good investments, performing the necessary due diligence, and selling when the investments reached maturity. I've earned a good income out of many projects and made landbanking my career. As president and CEO of Land Resources Investments, Inc., I've helped thousands of small investors profit in venture after venture.

But even someone with my vast experience still is afflicted with *Shoulda, coulda, wish I woulda.*

There are investments I wish I'd gotten into, but either backed off from because of a red flag, or didn't have the time to commit to adequately examine the project, or had my money tied up elsewhere and couldn't jump in.

This is true of investors in every field — whether they invest in real estate, the stock market, the commodities market, businesses, collectibles or what have you. Opportunities are passed over that later make them wish they hadn't. As the saying goes, "Hindsight is 20/20."

Rielly Morton Reynolds, a wise man I knew, told me that the biggest financial mistake he ever made was selling his real estate. He'd owned a great many properties and sold a great many and done quite well. But there were times when he didn't need to sell a particular property; he could have afforded to hold — and the profit he ended up with wasn't that spectacular. He especially regretted selling one particular property, which he characterized as his "$100 million mistake."

This property was a complex of buildings with 400 apartments in San Jose, California. It had become a headache to manage, and so Rielly had let it go. The biggest burden had been the 32 swim pools. He tired of their upkeep.

After he sold those apartment houses, their value skyrocketed. The San Jose area's population boomed. In fact, it continues to grow. Although my friend became quite wealthy, he could have become much, much wealthier had he kept that property.

Shoulda, coulda, wish I woulda.

Anyone who has seen someone else's investment go up in value usually suffers from this syndrome. Here's how it often happens: A piece of property catches your eye. You pass by it time and again in the course of your daily life. You see the property is for sale. And then someone buys it, and you notice that its value goes up. Another typical example is having been presented a piece of property to buy a few years back and having declined it . . . and today a shopping mall is sitting on it.

Driving by, you say, "Shoulda, coulda, wish I woulda."

Over-researchers suffer remorse, too

INVESTOR'S REMORSE AFFLICTS THE spectrum of investors. It even afflicts those plagued by analysis paralysis (as described in Chapter Eight), whose penchant for researching and questioning an investment almost always becomes an end in itself, without a committal to (or rejection of) the project.

Analysis paralysis is at the opposite end of the spectrum from blind investing — impulsively tossing money into an investment as a gamble based on a tip or hunch, or based on an ill-conceived sense of optimism (as described in Chapter Four). Either practice — analysis paralysis or blind investing — is foolhardy. The latter often wastes money, although it doesn't waste time, since it neglects the homework necessary to make an intelligent investment. The former doesn't waste money, but does waste time. Either tendency, though, is likely to result in investor's remorse.

If a project the over-researcher has analyzed (and re-analyzed) without investing in does pan out, this investor (or, rather, non-investor) will regret not putting the money down.

The blind investor will prove the saying, "A fool and his money are soon parted."

Shoulda, coulda, wish I woulda.

133

Taking solace in new opportunities

THE WAY I COMBAT my feelings of investor's remorse when I see a missed opportunity make someone else a profit is by telling myself, "Well, I bought this other piece instead. And that will make me a profit."

I remind myself there always are new opportunities down the road, always chances to make a killing. I congratulate myself for passing over projects that would have cost me money or made me very little.

I also remember that no one bats 1.000. But the good news is that if you keep on getting up to the plate, aggressively and intelligently going after what look like good pitches and avoiding the bad ones, you'll get a base hit. And sometimes you'll even hit a homer.

But if you quit the game, or never swing when you're at bat, you'll never even get on base.

And all you'll be left to say is, "Shoulda, coulda, wish I woulda."

Twelve Long Years Finally Deliver a Profit — but if Only the Investors Waited Just a Bit Longer!

It was a buyer's market in Palmdale, California, in 1990 when Pat Sheehan joined a group of a dozen investors to purchase 28 lots zoned for residential development within the city limits. In the 1980s, much of the buildable acreage in this community northeast of Los Angeles had been subdivided and sold to builders and developers. But then the expected growth hadn't materialized. Government orders dried up for Southern California defense contractors, which hurt the region's economy. So — with the slowdown in homebuilding — the homebuilders were selling off parcels at bargain rates.

The 28 lots Sheehan's group purchased in 1990 at $7,000 apiece were each

7,000 square feet. Their proposed subdivision had a tentative map. The investors' goal was to play a smart waiting game. They'd landbank the lots and eventually sell them off to builders after the market picked up again. It seemed like a good, safe investment to Sheehan, who was no novice to real estate; he was, and is, a land developer and homebuilding contractor. His Sheehan Construction, based in San Jose, California, is successful in buying land and building custom houses one or two at a time. He had connections in the land-investing field, and one connection was a Realtor who brought Sheehan into the Palmdale deal.

Then something unpredictable happened: The Palmdale housing market stayed down. Through the 1990s, there wasn't any appreciable demand. It was so bad, in fact, that banks foreclosed on houses whose owners couldn't make mortgage payments, and put these houses back on the market, creating a glut. Banks also foreclosed on a fair number of lots that builders had invested in; the builders didn't even get a chance to put houses on many of these lots.

The investors in Sheehan's group grew weary and discouraged. They knew they were stuck in the deal for the long haul. Whenever their 28 lots were listed on the market, no offers came. As Sheehan characterizes Palmdale's growth, with understatement: "It didn't develop as quickly as people thought it would."

FINALLY, IN 2002, LAND activity began to pick up. Bank foreclosures diminished. Housing sales were finally on the upswing. Offers trickled in to Sheehan's investment group for the 28 lots. By now, 12 years into the deal, members were anxious to get out — to sell while the demand persisted.

"No one knew how far it was going to go, or how long it was going to last, and felt it was time to move on," Sheehan says.

The first solid offer was for $15,000 per lot. That would more than double the investment. The group accepted. It was a typical reaction, Sheehan says, to a long-held investment that can finally be resolved.

"People get tired of it and want to move on. Their funds are needed for some other purpose. There is relief to get out. Especially if you finally see a profit in it."

Sheehan, though, sensed that Palmdale's market was set to soar. He attempted to take over the lots and build them out. Unfortunately, he lacked both the financial backing and the track record of managing such a large undertaking. "I was a little too late and it had already been sold," he says. "But it would've worked."

His instincts about Palmdale's market proved right. The market, after two decades of flatness, boomed. The value of the 28 lots quadrupled over the purchase price, to at least $60,000 each.

Sheehan's reaction?

A little bit of lingering regret. But he takes the what-might-have-been in stride. That's the only sane approach to the land-investment game, he says.

"We move on. Don't worry about that. Anyone who's owned property around California has seen it do a lot of different things."

Indeed, why brood? The Palmdale venture *did* turn a profit. "My particular investment on that was through my IRA account, and did a lot better than it would have done in the stock market," Sheehan says.

THE PROFIT FROM THE Palmdale deal, plus the experience and contacts with other landbankers he met from that deal, led Sheehan to invest in acreage in nearby Lancaster, on which 16 homes were built. Just by getting into the game in Southern California led to more investment possibilities. Action begat action.

In sum, Sheehan says, "You can always learn something from each project, good and bad."

Secondly, you should never complain if you've made money on a project — even if it doesn't end up being as much as if you'd held it longer and the value went higher.

"I don't know who can predict that," Sheehan says, philosophically.

"Maybe it would be a good idea to sell off part of your holdings at a profit and see how the rest does."

But, again, who's to say the rest of it won't tank?

Unpredictable. Anyway, there's always the next deal.

KEY POINTS TO REMEMBER:

- Investor's remorse — characterized by the exclamation, "Shoulda, coulda, wish I woulda"— afflicts all investors, and can come from selling too soon, passing on an opportunity that ended up profiting someone else, or lacking the resources to seize a promising investment.
- The avid landbanker can take consolation in the facts that no investor gets all the good deals, and opportunities will always be out there.

CONCLUSION

Congratulations on reaching the end of this book!

You deserve credit for investing the time and effort to absorb the essentials of landbanking, And trust me: You will reap the rewards. For you have now put distance between yourself and the majority of investors and would-be investors in land.

You have gained knowledge that they don't have, and which I didn't have, but surely could have used, when I embarked on my first land purchase at the tender age of 21. You have absorbed information that will help you recognize a good deal from a poor one, and help you know when to buy and when to sell. You have put yourself closer to hitting pay dirt.

If this was your first reading of the book, I recommend that you reread it at your leisure, and then keep it handy as a reference guide as you progress in your landbanking career. Also, when you do hit pay dirt, feel free to contact me at darren@landbanknation.com. We may print your success story in a subsequent edition of this book. Your story could well inspire another worthy investor to pursue profitable landbanking.

NOW FOR A FEW words of inspiration:

The biggest obstacle to your first landbanking investment is likely more *psychological* than financial. So remember, and take to heart, what was said in Chapter Seven: A wise strategy is focusing first on finding a great piece of land, *then* working on coming up with the financing.

Maybe there are other psychological barriers to making your first land purchase. Perhaps you're still struggling with whether you really need to invest in land. Perhaps you're letting a naysayer discourage you, or your spouse isn't entirely sold on the enterprise. The lessons contained in this book should suffice to steel your spirit.

Please know this: Success resides on the other side of fear. Shakespeare put it this way in the dialogue of one of his plays[45]:

"Our doubts are traitors, and make us lose the good we oft might win by fearing to attempt."

It is now your time to dare to attempt. To find a sound landbanking investment. To win the good.

To hit **PAY DIRT**!

---

[45] From *Measure by Measure*, Act I, Scene 4.

About Land Resource Investments, Inc.

Land Resource Investments, Inc., is a landbank-development company incorporated in California and headquartered in Sparks, Nevada (next to Reno).

LRI, of which I am president and CEO, is unique in the landbanking industry. LRI finds large, quality pre-development parcels in the paths of urban growth — and shows groups of individuals and small investors how they can invest in these choice parcels.

The benefit for investors is that they can compete for large pieces of valuable land against the traditional players — big corporations and other ultra-wealthy investors — who previously were the only parties able to purchase such prime real estate.

LRI continues to research new opportunities, not only in California but other Western states. LRI performs all the legwork on a project — carefully finding pre-development real estate with high potential in the path of urban growth, conducting thorough due diligence, recruiting investors, buying and managing the property.[46] Investors, enjoying the leverage gained from being part of a big investment, earn a profit on their percentage after the parcel matures and is sold

---

[46] The Cooleys, who authored *The Simple Truth about Western Land Investment*, had this message for investors starting out in landbanking: "You don't have to do it alone — in fact we think it is foolish to try to — for the same reason that it would be foolish for you to try to teach yourself to fly an airplane."

(typically to a land developer or home builder).

The western United States is a fantastic market in which to landbank profitably. This is because its phenomenal historical growth — with land prices increasing for the past century — shows no sign of waning, given the continual increase in population and expansions of infrastructure and highways, industry and support services. Therefore, most of LRI's efforts are in the western United States.[47]

LRI's investments are attractive to people investing for retirement. An individual who accumulated assets in a 401(k) retirement fund with an employer, but has left that employer, can roll over the funds into a self-directed Individual Retirement Account. Also, an investor usually can roll over profits from a real estate sale into an LRI investment, since the reinvestment will be into what the federal government considers a "like-kind property." (This is known as a "1031 rollover" or a "Starker exchange.")

TO ENCAPSULATE:

- The entry prices for large parcels of prime landbanking real estate are almost always out of the financial reach of individual investors. They traditionally have been forced to pursue less desirable parcels that are smaller and, often, further from paths of urban growth, and take longer to mature.
- Even individual investors, with moderate income or capital, are able to leverage their investments by buying into a lucrative parcel they otherwise couldn't afford.
- LRI finds large undeveloped parcels in prime paths of urban growth. The western United States' residential population is increasing due to a combination of the birth rate exceeding the mortality rate, and immigration outpacing emigration. Therefore, the pressure for developing land continues.

---

[47] The Cooleys, writing in the 1960s, said, "Trying to stop the present runaway migration to the western region of the United States is like trying to stem an avalanche." Their words were borne out by the subsequent population explosion, which continues.

- LRI is experienced in locating property around medium-size cities that have quickly expanding populations, a robust homebuilding demand and identifiable and verifiable paths of growth.

- LRI selects properties that are within a fast-growing city's sphere of influence, as identified by the city's general plan. Furthermore, the properties are within eyeshot of new buildings or housing subdivisions, and within serviceable, functional and practical distance to power, water and sewer lines.

- Each LRI project undergoes an extensive approval process with the state government. The Department of Real Estate issues a report on each LRI project.

- LRI's expertise is used to purchase the property, advertise it at the peak of the market, and sell the property for maximum profit.

- Investors who qualify can roll over 401(k) funds or real estate profits into LRI investments.

CONTACTING LAND RESOURCE INVESTMENTS, INC.

Land Resource Investments, Inc.'s, website contains a great deal of information about landbanking opportunities:
www.LandBankNation.com.

Investors also can call the toll-free number: (800) 628-9946, or fax a request for information to (775) 358-4464.

Glossary

Terms in Real Estate Development

ACRE: A measure equal to 43,560 square feet.

AGENT (REAL ESTATE): A person licensed by the state to carry on the business of dealing in real estate. An agent may receive a commission for his or her part in bringing together a buyer and seller, or parties to an exchange.

APPRAISAL: An opinion o f value based upon a factual analysis.

APPRECIATION: An increased value of property due to either a positive improvement of the area or the elimination of negative factors.

ARTICLES OF INCORPORATION: Documentation filed with the state that sets forth general information about a corporation. More specific rules of the corporation would be contained in its bylaws.

ASSESSED VALUE: Value placed upon property for property-tax purposes by the tax assessor.

ANNUAL: By the year.

BIRTH RATE: The number of births in a given area during a given period of time, based on per-thousand population.

BOUNDARY: A separation, natural or artificial, that marks the division of two contiguous properties.

BROKER (REAL ESTATE): A person licensed by the state (as is an agent) to carry on the business of dealing in real estate, and who has taken an additional test to be able to run a private firm. (See definition for "agent.")

BROKER'S PRICE OPINION. "BPO" for short, it's given by a real estate broker about a property, but is not as thorough, and may not be as accurate, as a real estate appraiser's report. The broker may provide the BPO for free, expecting the buyer's business.

BUYER'S MARKET: A market condition favoring the buyer.

BYLAWS: Rules and regulations, adopted by an association or corporation, that govern its activities.

CC&R'S (COVENANTS, CONDITIONS AND RESTRICTIONS): A term used in some areas to describe the restrictive limitations that may be placed on private property. Another term is "deed codes." Often set by homeowners' associations, they can be more restrictive than city ordinances, and because they are private contracts they can ban acts that otherwise would be constitutionally protected. Examples: Structures may be painted only in earth tones; no more than three vehicles owned by the occupant are allowed on the occupant's property; no motor homes may be parked on the curb more than 24 hours; no political signage is allowed in the front yard; no garage sales are permitted except for the once-a-year date set for the subdivision).

CLOSING: In real estate sales, the final procedure in which documents are executed and/or recorded, and the sale is legally completed.

CODE OF ETHICS: A code of professional standards containing aspects of fairness, and duty to the profession and the general public.

DEPARTMENT OF REAL ESTATE: That department of the state government responsible for the licensing and regulation of persons engaged in the real estate business. The person heading the department is usually called the real estate commissioner.

DIRECTIONAL GROWTH: The path of growth of an urban area. Used to determine where and when future development will be most profitable.

DIVERSIFY: To spread out investments among different types of investments and markets (such as real estate, stocks and bonds) to ensure balance and diminish risks.

DUE DILIGENCE: The process of investigating details of a potential investment.

ECONOMIC CYCLE: Also known as a "business cycle," the pattern of business activity running through the four phases of expansion, prosperity, contraction and recession (or depression). These cycles repeat.

ENGINEERING COMPANY: A company hired by a land owner or developer to perform services that include subdivision, land-use planning, circulation plan, infrastructure and utilities plan, landscape plan, fiscal impact analysis, land survey, preliminary and final site planning, preparation and submittal of a tentative map, and final maps for approval by governmental agencies.

ENTITLEMENTS: The granting of certain rights to specific property by governmental agencies, including zoning, tentative subdivision map, final subdivision map and building permits.

EQUITY: The market value of real property, less the amount of existing liens. Also: Any ownership investment (such as stocks, bonds or real estate).

ESCROW: Documents and/or money or other valuables deposited with a neutral third party (such as an escrow agent or company) to be released and delivered upon fulfillment of the conditions of an agreement (typically, a written sales contract) between a buyer and seller.

ENVIRONMENTAL IMPACT REPORT (EIR): A report required by governmental agencies related to the probable effect a subdivision development will have on the surrounding area (environment). The report is prepared by an independent company to federal, state or local guidelines.

ENVIRONMENTAL SITE ASSESSMENT (ESA): An assessment of the environmental condition of a site, often performed by an engineering consulting company, to determine whether the land's soil and topography, and location and zoning allow construction on the land, and whether hazards such as contamination exist. Most lenders require ESAs before making a loan on a property.

FEASIBILITY STUDY: A study of an area, before the purchase or development of a property, to determine the probable financial success of the venture.

FEE SIMPLE: An estate under which the owner is entitled to unrestricted powers to dispose of the property, and which can be left by a will or inherited.

FINAL SUBDIVISION MAP (FINAL MAP): The subdivision map prepared by an engineering company that has received final approval from all interested governmental agencies in order to establish a subdivision of a specific property. When the map is recorded, it becomes the basis for the legal description of the subdivided property, including individual lots.

FINISHED LOTS: Lots in a subdivision with an approved final subdivision map, suitable for construction. Off-site improvements can include sidewalks, curbs, streets, sewer, utilities and streetlights. A builder can start construction without further improvements or approvals other than a building permit.

FREE AND CLEAR: Real property against which there are no liens, especially voluntary liens (loans).

FULL DISCLOSURE: The revealing of all the known facts that may affect the decision of a buyer. A broker must disclose known defects in the property for sale.

GENERAL CONTRACTOR: A person who contracts for the construction of an entire building or project, rather than for a portion of the work. The general contractor coordinates all the work, and is responsible for payment to the said subcontractors, such as carpenters, electricians, plumbers and roofers.

GENERAL PARTNER: A co-owner of a business who is liable for all debts and obligations of the business, and responsible for the management and operation of the partnership. The general partner can have control of the business and take actions binding on the other partners.

GOVERNMENTAL AGENCIES: All regulatory bodies at the city, county or state level that control or issue permits to sub-dividers, developers or builders. The bodies can include a planning department, city council, county commission building department, road department and public works department.

GRANT DEED: A type of deed used to transfer real property. It contains warranties against prior conveyances or encumbrances.

GRID SYSTEM: The system used in the United States since the nation's founding to locate property on maps. The grid system shows "townships" (each of which equal 36 square miles); "sections" (each of which equal 1 square mile, or 640 acres); "location plats" (which divide sections into quarters — a northeast, northwest, southeast and southwest quarter); and "parcels" (each of which are one-sixty-fourth of 160 acres — or 2 1/2 acres). Townships are shown on a squared survey grid. The coordinates run north and south from a horizontal "base line," and "ranges" run east and west along a vertical "meridian line." (See illustrations)

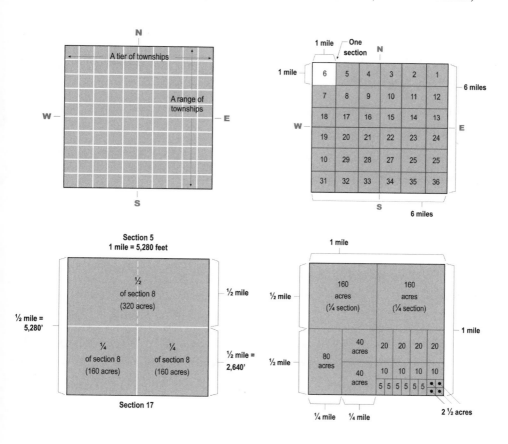

Top left: States are divided into townships, each of which is 36 square miles.

Top right: Townships are divided into 36 sections, each of which is one square mile (640 acres).

Bottom left: Sections are quartered into location plats (160 acres each), referred to by northwest, northeast, southwest or southeast quarter.

Bottom right: Sections are divided all the way down into 2½-acre parcels.

INFLATION: The increase in prices in an economy above its natural growth.

INFRASTRUCTURE: Services and facilities necessary to communities. Examples: streets, bridges, public transportation, utility generation and delivery.

INVENTORY: Land or lots owned or controlled by a developer or builder. Inventory can be any or all of the following: raw/undeveloped land, pre-development land, pre-builder land, finished lots.

INVESTMENT PROPERTY: Generally, any property purchased for the primary purpose of profit. The profit may be from income or resale.

LANDBANKING: The process of buying and holding land for future sale or development.

LEGAL DESCRIPTION: A method of geographically identifying a parcel of land. Two descriptions commonly are used. One description is an assessor's parcel number, which can be found on a property-tax bill, and is based on the common gridded survey system. The other description is from the "indiscriminate metes and bounds system," which is prevalent in parts of the southern United States, and describes a plot in terms of its location to neighboring landowners, trees, rocks and streams.

LETTER OF INTENT: A preliminary agreement from a potential buyer stating the proposed terms for a final contract to buy a property. Typically, the buyer agrees in the letter to put a certain sum of money (refundable up to a certain period) into an escrow account while completing due diligence on the property. The letter is not an official offer and creates no obligation.

LEVERAGE: The use of borrowed money to enhance one's speculative capacity for profit. *Example: An investor borrows $80,000 at 5 percent interest and puts down $20,000 of his own money to buy a $100,000 property. The property increases in value by 20 percent — to $120,000. The buyer sells the property and pays off the loan ($80,000 plus the $4,000 in interest) and comes away with a $36,000 profit. The investor has leveraged a debt-to-equity ratio of 4:1 to enjoy a 180 percent profit on his personal investment of $20,000.*

MANAGING PARTNER: A partner in a business (or investment) who is active

150

in the day-to-day operations of the partnership, and can be legally empowered and charged with managing the business/investment. Often, a general partner is the managing partner, too.

MEGALOPOLIS: A heavily populated, continuous urban area including many cities.

MORATORIUM: In reference to building homes, a governmental halt on home construction to slow the rate of development. Typically, the number of building permits issued is drastically restricted.

NET PROFIT: Profit remaining after the deduction of all expenses from income for a given period. Generally classified as either net before taxes, or net after taxes.

OPEN SPACE: Land use designated for agriculture, recreation, scenic beauty, natural resources, watershed or wildlife.

PAPER LOTS: Lots shown on an approved tentative subdivision map. The "paper" lots do not have a recorded, individual-lot legal description, and exist only on the map (on paper).

PATH OF GROWTH: An identifiable direction (path) in which a city, town or metropolitan area is growing, wherein specific property will be affected by development (residential, commercial or industrial) in a reasonably short period of time.

PLANNING DEPARTMENT: A board or department within a city, county or similar local government entity that must approve of proposed subdivision or development projects. The planning department recommends approval or rejection of subdivisions or developments to a higher board such as a city council or a county board of commissioners or supervisors, which will give final approval or rejection of plans for a property.

PLANNING STAFF: The salaried employees working within the planning department of a local government. The staff, which can include engineers and environmental experts, reviews the development projects and makes recommendations to the sub-divider/developer and to the planning department.

PRE-DEVELOPMENT LAND: Land, located in the growth path of a city or metropolitan area, that has been governmentally zoned for its intended use (such as single-family residences, multi-unit housing, commercial retail) and has received governmental approval of basic entitlements or zoning.

PRELIMINARY SUBDIVISION MAP (PRELIMINARY MAP): A draft of the proposed tentative map prepared by an engineering firm for submittal to the appropriate governmental planning staff for review and suggestions prior to submittal of the application for tentative-map approval.

PRELIMINARY TITLE REPORT: A report from a title company proving that the seller is the property's rightful owner, and listing any debtor claims against the property, such as for income or property taxes. The title company gives the report before the transaction goes to closing, when the title company will issue the title policy to the property.

PRESCRIPTIVE EASEMENT: An easement (right to use another's land for a stated purpose) against someone else's real property, acquired by continual use of the easement without the owner's permission for a period of time specified by state law to establish the easement. *Examples: A landowner running an irrigation ditch through a neighbor's property; a pedestrian using a shortcut through a property, thus establishing a right-of-way.* (Prescriptive easements do not show up on title reports and the precise location and/or use of the easement is not necessarily clear and can move because of practice or erosion.)

PROPERTY REPORT: A report that includes a property's assessed value, legal description, lot size, mortgage, ownership, sales history and often other crucial information.

PROSPECTUS: A formal document listing or outlining the chief features and facts about a venture, including risks to the investor.

PRORATE: To divide, distribute or assess proportionately.

PUBLIC REPORT: A state can issue a public report on properties within a planned subdivision. The report would contain any warnings given by a city or county government about the properties.

REALTOR: A licensed real estate professional who is a member of the National Association of Realtors. "Realtor" is capitalized.

RATE OF RETURN: The annual percentage of return, both of and on invested capital.

SPECULATIVE LAND: Land purchased for resale rather than any other use by the buyer, such as for development.

SPHERE OF INFLUENCE: An unincorporated area designated in a city's master plan as territory into which the city will extend its legal borders, and thus provide services and tax residents. In the sense of human relationships, the term refers to all the people whom an individual personally knows and deals with regularly.

SUPPLY AND DEMAND: The economic theory that when supply exceeds demand, prices fall, and when demand exceeds supply, prices rise.

1031 EXCHANGE: A tax-deferral strategy allowed under Section 1031 of the Internal Revenue Code by which a property seller, complying with the strict guidelines of the code, rolls over profit from a land sale by reinvesting it into a property of equal or greater value. Also known as a Starker exchange.

TENANCY IN COMMON: An undivided ownership in real estate by two or more persons. The interest need not be equal and, in the event of the death of one of the owners, no right of survivorship in the other owners exists.

TENTATIVE SUBDIVISION MAP (TENTATIVE MAP): A map submitted to the appropriate governmental agencies by an engineering firm on behalf of a sub-divider. The map has met all the governmental requirements, and its approval is conditioned upon completion of the requirements set forth in the development agreement by and between the developer and the appropriate governmental agencies.

TITLE: A legal document evidencing a party's ownership of or right to a property.

TITLE COMPANY: A company specializing in investigating ownership titles to a property, and also insuring titles for lenders (through lender's policies) and owners (through owner's policies).

TITLE INSURANCE: Insurance, purchased from a title company, against loss resulting from defects of title (such as liens or other outstanding claims) to a specifically described parcel of real property.

UNDEVELOPED LAND (RAW LAND): Land in its natural state. Land that has not qualified for the basic entitlements of zoning or for a tentative subdivision map. Usually located outside of the city limits and urban-service area.

UNDIVIDED INTEREST DEVELOPMENT: A development, such as a condominium complex or community apartment house, in which there is property (such as yards and driveways) owned in common, apart from separate interests (such as individual housing units).

UNENCUMBERED: Free of liens and other encumbrances. Free and clear.

UNIT: One of any group.

URBAN SPRAWL: The spreading of urban developments (such as houses, shopping centers or office parks) on undeveloped land near a city. A synonym is "suburbanization."

YIELD: Ratio of income from an investment to the total cost of the investment over a given period of time.

ZONING: The division of a city or county by legislative regulations into areas (zones), specifying the uses allowable for the real property (land) located within these areas. Uses are usually in one of the four following categories: residential, multi-family, commercial, industrial.

Share Your Success Story

If you have a success story in land investing, I'd love to hear from you. Please feel free to email me at **paydirt@LandBankNation.com.**

If accepted, your story may appear in a subsequent edition of this book.

— Darren K. Proulx

About the Author

Darren K. Proulx lives with his wife and six children in northern Nevada.

A volunteer in his community and church, Proulx (ryhmes with true) has served as a Cub Scout and Boy Scout leader, and has been a reserve deputy sheriff.

He is president and CEO of Land Resource Investments, Inc., and publisher of *Land Investment News*.

To date, Proulx has been directly involved in real estate deals worth more than $50 million, benefiting more than 1,500 investors.

Pay Dirt is his first book.

For More Information on
Land Resource Investments, Inc.

Please visit **www.LandBankNation.com**.
Or call toll-free: (800) 628-9946.